CREEDS, CODES AND COWBOY COMMANDMENTS

TV's B-Western Heroes
Rules to Live By

Matthew McKenzie

Scripture quotations marked (ESV) are from the ESV® Bible (The Holy Bible, English Standard Version®), copyright © 2001 by Crossway, a publishing ministry of Good News Publishers. Used by permission. All rights reserved.

Scripture quotations marked (NLT) are taken from the Holy Bible, New Living Translation, copyright ©1996, 2004, 2007, 2013, 2015 by Tyndale House Foundation. Used by permission of Tyndale House Publishers, Inc., Carol Stream, Illinois 60188. All rights reserved.

Scripture quotations marked (KJV) are taken from the King James Version of the Bible.

Scripture quotations marked (NASB) are taken from the New American Standard Bible® (NASB), Copyright © 1960, 1962, 1963, 1968, 1971, 1972, 1973, 1975, 1977, 1995 by The Lockman Foundation. Used by permission. www.Lockman.org

Unless otherwise noted, all images, illustrations and photographs used are from the author's personal collection.

Opposite page: quotation taken from character dialogue in the episode, "Smoking Guns," of *The Roy Rogers Show*.

ISBN-13: 978-0692832776

"Keeping our young people on the right path is more important than gold."

\-   Dale Evans

DEDICATION

To my family

CONTENTS

ACKNOWLEDGMENTS

It is possible that my enjoyment and appreciation for stories of the American West originated, at least in part, in time spent with my paternal grandfather. He lived in a small town in southern Illinois, but was normally seen wearing a western-styled shirt, cowboy boots and a Stetson cowboy hat. I can fondly recall his regaling my brothers and me with stories of his father, who was a real-life cowboy in Oklahoma Territory at the end of the 19th century. He was also an avid reader of Zane Grey novels and a faithful viewer of television westerns like *Gunsmoke* and *Bonanza*. One of my more memorable Christmas gifts received as a young child was the dual cap-pistols and holster set he presented to each of my three brothers and me.

In the past few years, I have been privileged to attend several Western Film-themed festivals. At those events, I have found that many of the exhibitors and vendors are not only subject matter experts for western films and western television series, but are invariably generous with their time and are willing to discuss these topics at length with total strangers. Those conversations were certainly helpful in guiding my research for this book.

I would like to express my appreciation to my wife and children for their patience and understanding as I reviewed hundreds of episodes of early television western programs. I especially want to thank my wife for her support and encouragement in the whole process. Finally, I am grateful to those who reviewed the book and offered their feedback and encouragement.

PREFACE

In the following manner was a week of television programming summarized in the October 18, 1954 issue of *TIME* magazine:

> The good guys on TV last week were, as usual, giving the bad guys their lumps. As millions of youngsters watched in beady-eyed fascination, Roy Rogers (with the help of Dale and Trigger) got the drop on some slow-witted fur thieves; Hopalong Cassidy (with help from his younger brother) corralled a batch of badmen who had holed up in a gold mine; the Lone Ranger (with help from Tonto and his horse Silver) outwitted a pseudo-Englishman and won an inheritance which —naturally —he promptly donated to a worthy cause. Meanwhile, out in the cold reaches of outer space, a band of interstellar cavemen were put to flight just as they were about to burn alive Vena, the beautiful navigator for Rocky Jones, Space Ranger; a bearded, mad scientist was certain to be thwarted by right-thinking Captain Video who, as the press release puts it, is an unbeatable "combination of Einstein, King Arthur and Marco Polo," and Space Patrol's Commander Buzz Corry was zooming through the cosmos intent on reforming the almost limitless supply of villains with his soul-washing Brain-O-Graph. (*TIME*, October 18, 1954).

Indeed, in the early days of television, there were plenty of heroes regularly going about their business of thwarting evil on screen for the amusement of adults and children alike, but the most popular type of hero was the western cowboy. This may be surprising to some readers, but in reviewing the history of television's beginnings, it can be seen that western programming was actually the foundation on which television grew as a commercially viable medium. In a 1950 article in the trade magazine, *Sponsor*, the irony of the supremacy of westerns was duly noted:

> In this, the era of nuclear fission, wonder drugs, and super-complicated political ideology, the simple salty, and down-to-earth legend of the American cowboy thrives as it never has before. That, for anybody's money, is the greatest single tribute imaginable to the power of the broadcast media. For it was television (aided by radio)

that bucked the tide of sophistication and turned the nation's kids into one mad posse of ten-gallon hat wearing, cap-gun packing plainsmen. (*Sponsor*, September 25, 1950).

The cowboy as "hero" preceded television, having already been a highly successful genre in the movies for decades. However, television allowed even wider access to the cowboy heroes, connecting with audiences who for various reasons had not patronized the movie theaters. As we shall see, the impact of television's western heroes on the American culture was enormous.

Then, as now, it was natural for children to want heroes - someone they could look up to, even imitate. For many children in the viewing audience, daily life involved facing obstacles that were bigger than them: long-term illnesses, debilitating injuries, dysfunctional families, lack of comfortable living accommodations, and so on. Thus, they could in some ways identify themselves with a hero who likewise was taking on bigger-than-themselves challenges. Beyond life on-screen, when a hero like Roy Rogers visited a children's hospital or an orphanage, it was easy for a child to see him as an authentic, accessible hero. When the Lone Ranger talked to them about investing in their country through the purchase of U.S. Saving Stamps, they could feel like they were part of this hero's "team" for their common good. The question seems less one of "do children have heroes," and more a question of "how does one become a hero to children."

How does a character – real or fictional – get to be a hero in the public's eye? Early television programming presented near-perfect cowboy heroes for the viewing audience – especially children. Several of these cowboy heroes had their own published rules to live by, with titles for their rules that used words like "creed," "code," "rules," "pledge," "oath," or even "cowboy commandments." This book will explore the integral part that a character's set of values – and therefore, the things the hero claims to champion – played in setting up that character as a hero in the public conscience.

The development and adoption by a group of a "creed" of some sort to which that group claims to adhere is likely a familiar idea to many readers. Well-known organizations such as the Boy Scouts of America have their points of the Boy Scout Law (a Scout is trustworthy, loyal, helpful, friendly, courteous, kind, obedient, cheerful, thrifty, brave, clean, and reverent) and their Boy Scout Slogan ("Do a Good Turn Daily!"). The author is familiar with his own boyhood, church-based boys' program, Royal Rangers, which had its own code (the points of the Royal Ranger Code included a Ranger was to be alert, clean, honest, courageous, loyal, courteous, obedient, and spiritual) and pledge (which included each Ranger's intent "to make the Golden Rule my daily rule"). The points included in many such creeds tend to be similar in spirit, differing mostly in semantics.

Not only did each of several early television western heroes publish their rules by which to live, but the format in which they were publicized typically comprised a list of ten points. That the list had ten points likely resonates with many of us today (as it did fans back in the 1950s) as an invocation of the Ten Commandments in the Bible's Old Testament. It was this observation that led to the central themes of this book: first, to demonstrate the connection between the codes and creeds of television's B western cowboy heroes and a higher authority – specifically, the teachings found in the Bible; and secondly, to challenge us today – especially parents – to consider what and whose values do our contemporary "heroes" claim to embrace?

It is not my intent herein to recruit new fans of old television shows, nor do I suggest that heroes must necessarily be of the western type. However, it is my hope that upon reading this book, the reader will in the future give more thought to the values embraced by their heroes and the origin of the principles on which their heroes base their sense of right and wrong.

Creeds, Codes and Cowboy Commandments

INTRODUCTION

Fans of *The Andy Griffith Show* may recall an episode in season six, in which promoter Fred Gibson brings to Mayberry his Wild West show, featuring its star attraction, Clarence Earp – a direct descendent of the legendary Wyatt Earp, according to Gibson. In the story, Gibson prompts Clarence to challenge some of the local men into various wrestling-type matches in order to validate the claims of Clarence's fighting abilities. The young boys of Mayberry love the images and exploits associated with the Western hero, and take to heart Gibson's proclamation that Clarence follows the Code of the West: "the man who can fight is the man who is right." When the boys later need to settle an argument among themselves, they choose to fight as a way of settling their dispute. After Sheriff Andy Taylor interrupts their fight, they cite Gibson's version of the Code of the West as the reason for their choosing to fight. Andy's reaction seemed to be twofold. He was frustrated that the boys had adopted Gibson's version of the Code of the West, and he was worried about the extent to which the boys might continue to act out what they have seen in Gibson's traveling Wild West show.

The episode illustrates two key themes that will be explored in this book: the stated "Code of the West" adhered to by a Western hero whose target audience was youthful, and the concern of parents (and other authority figures like teachers) about the values by which their children are influenced. While the "man who can fight" may certainly make for lively entertainment, how does one know if he "is the one who is right?" Since the "bad guys" in a story can also fight, there has to be some other way of discerning who "is right."

In every person there seems to be an innate sense of the existence of "right" and "wrong" (even if what constitutes right versus wrong may differ between groups of people). Perhaps this may explain the universal and enduring popularity of heroes in everything from the Marvel Comics universe to the appeal of the murder mystery story in its various forms – novels, movies, TV series, radio shows, and more. We all want to see justice upheld. We wish to see the triumph of "right" over "wrong" and look for "heroes" who can bring about said triumph. This usually involves the need for the hero to fight in the process of upholding justice, which makes for popular, action-based entertainment. However, it is a more satisfying entertainment when the audience can agreeably identify with the values on which the hero is acting.

Americans have always embraced the heroic figure fighting against the odds for a just cause. Christopher Langley, executive director and historian at the Lone Pine Film History Museum, was quoted in an article in a 2013 issue of *American Cowboy*:

> I think we, as an American culture, have really identified with that. The lone savior and his sidekick standing up for the community against the bad guys, fighting for what's right. To square things that are wrong. That really appeals to us—heroes who, no matter what, have a code of behavior and follow it. They stand up against the enemy, even if they have to do it alone. (*American Cowboy*, retrieved January 12, 2015 from AmericanCowboy.com).

While the focus of this book will be the Western hero as seen in early television programming, much of what is discussed is also applicable to other "hero" types. Does the hero (whether cowboy, detective, medical/scientific genius, law enforcement official, or super-hero) have a code of behavior? Can the hero be observed to abide by it? What assumptions or values underlay the hero's code?

Many readers may not be aware of just how popular the cowboy hero was in American culture not so long ago. Even as some other heroes had already been established in the American pop culture scene (several real-life military heroes, and fictional heroes like the Hardy Boys, Superman and numerous other super-heroes), in the early years of television it was the American Western hero who captured the imaginations and admiration of millions of children and adults. Beginning with the edited-for-TV films of Hopalong Cassidy in 1948, the western became an integral part of TV programming for the first twenty or so years of television's history. By 1954, a writer for *TV Guide* admitted the obvious: "It is a general practice among so-called hep adults, including this writer, to sneer politely at the antics of what has come to be known as The Western Star. It has come to the attention of this desk, however, that we are all in the wrong pew and had better move over." ("Why Roy Rogers Is Cowboy King." *TV Guide*, July 17, 1954).

The sociological and psychological explanations for how and why the cowboy (in this book, the term "western hero" and "cowboy" will be used interchangeably) came to be a hero in American culture is beyond the scope of this book. It is enough to know that the cowboy as hero had been well established in American entertainment long before television programming began. Interestingly, in the American Heritage Dictionary, under "cowboy," the second definition listed – after being defined as a hired man who tends cattle and performs his work-related duties on horseback – is the cowboy as "an adventurous hero."

Over time, countless stories and legends came out of the lives and work of the cowboy of the American West – some true and some fictional. The idea of the cowboy being a hero was explained in the 1890s by G. A. Henty in the preface to one of his stories, in which he described the cowboys of the American West as "a body of men unrivalled in point of hardihood and devotion to work, as well as in reckless courage and wild daring." Basing his novel largely upon the first-hand accounts of the West given to him by "a near relative," Henty stated he had "given but a small proportion of the perilous adventures through which he went, for had I given them in full it would, I am sure, have seemed to you that the story was too improbable to be true. In treating of cow-boy life, indeed, it may well be said that truth is stranger than fiction." (Henty, *Redskin and Cow-Boy, A Tale of the Western Plains*, copyright 1891).

The popularity of cowboy stories continued from the late 1800s in novels and magazine serials into the next century, and expanded into the newer mediums of silent films, radio programs, comic books, newspaper comic strips, sound films, and television.

In this book, I hope to make the case that the early television cowboy heroes could make the claim to be fighting for justice and what is "right" on the basis of the ideals expressed in their creeds and codes. Rather than being right because they could fight (as the fictional Mr. Gibson asserted in his visit to Mayberry), the early TV western hero chose to fight only when that was the necessary course of action to uphold what was "right." That they could fight – with fists, guns, knives, etc. – made for entertaining, on-screen action, but that their behavior was motivated by a specific code of values and principles is what actually set them apart as heroes.

Creeds, Codes and Cowboy Commandments

1

CODES OF THE WEST

Young Robby Talbot had but one wish for Christmas – to be reunited with his father. While he and his mother, Mary Talbot, were working hard at home on their ranch, his father, Ben Talbot, had been away from them for quite some time, having gone off to prospect for gold in the mining camps. By now, Robby was missing his father terribly, and much preferred having his father present in their home to having more money. One day, the unexpected visit of two strangers – one masked, the other an Indian – gave Robby hope that perhaps his Christmas wish could come true.

The visitors were the Lone Ranger and Tonto. After a lengthy conversation, they were acquainted with Robby and his mother's circumstances and promised Robby they would search for the boy's father throughout the mining camps. As they prepared to leave the Talbot's home, the Lone Ranger spoke: "Ben Talbot has a misguided sense of values. He's lost, Tonto. If he can't find himself, maybe somebody else ought to try!"

Tonto agreed, adding, "Ah, boy say if father come home, it be best Christmas he and mother ever have."

"We're going to try to make that wish come true," said the Lone Ranger, as he and Tonto mounted their horses, Silver and Scout, and rode away from the Talbot ranch.

The Lone Ranger, using his 'old prospector' disguise, began to visit mining camps inquiring among the miners whether any of them knew of the whereabouts of Ben Talbot. Finally, at one of the mining camps, the Lone Ranger managed to find Ben. During their ensuing conversation, Ben seemed a bit agitated when the Lone Ranger spoke of Robby's desire to have the family reunited. The Lone Ranger pressed the point, "Just thought you'd like to hear from home. Ain't havin' much luck findin' gold, are ya?"

"I'll strike it . . . one of these days," Ben responded, with a note of weariness in his voice.

"When you do, Ben, think it'll make ya happier?" asked the Lone Ranger.

"I can give my family everything – all they've ever wanted," said Ben.

"All they want is you, Ben," said the Lone Ranger. "You ever think of that? By the time you find what you're lookin' for, that boy of yours goin' to be all growed up. Best part of havin' kids is watchin' 'em grow, develop into something you can be proud of! Too bad if you miss that."

Sensing that Ben was realizing the truth of his words, the Lone Ranger – still in his 'old prospector' disguise and voice – suggested to Ben that it was not too late for him to rejoin his family and raise his son. The Lone Ranger pointed out to Ben that if he left the mining camp immediately, he could even be home in time for Christmas. Ben decided that was the right thing to do, abandoned his search for gold, and returned home to stay, to the delight of Robby and Mary.

That story was told in "Christmas Story," a season five episode of *The Lone Ranger* television series, and originally broadcast in December, 1956. The story provides an example of how the Lone Ranger acted on his belief that an individual will be better off when living according to a well-guided set of values. The Lone Ranger made it his quest to not only locate Ben Talbot, the absent father, but to challenge Ben's thinking by causing him to reconsider his priorities and responsibilities.

Even before the television series, the Lone Ranger was a widely-known hero thanks to the highly-successful, long-running *Lone Ranger* radio program which had originally introduced him to the public in 1933. In the August, 1943, issue of *Radio Guide*, the Lone Ranger's status as a hero was attributed to more than just the marketing efforts of breakfast cereals and the image of a man and his horse. The article proposed his hero status and popularity was directly connected with the Lone Ranger's creed, a written set of values by which the Lone Ranger lived.

In addition to the Lone Ranger, several other B western cowboy heroes of 1950s television were known to have published a creed or cowboy code of their own. These were created to reinforce the image and ideals of each cowboy hero with their young audience – and parents. However, before delving into some of these cowboy creeds and codes, let us first review the origin of the more general idea of a "Code of the West."

In the days when cowboys and their herds of cattle freely roamed the plains and prairies of the frontier, there was generally no written law on the range. This led the cowboys and pioneers working the new land to develop their own rules of behavior which became known as the Code of the West. These "laws" were never formally written or codified into statutes, but represented agreement as to certain rules of conduct that were respected throughout the territories of the Old West.

The "laws" within the Code of the West, though unwritten, were more or less common knowledge to the cowboys and pioneers and they typically abided by it. The Code generally was comprised of rules that addressed things like fairness, respect for others' persons and property, respect for the land and its natural resources, and acceptable social behavior. Following is a list of some of the items included by Western historians as part of the Code of the West:

- Defend yourself whenever necessary;
- Don't make a threat without expecting dire consequences;
- Never pass anyone on the trail without saying "Howdy";
- When approaching someone from behind, give a loud greeting before you get within shooting range;
- After you pass someone on the trail, don't look back at him. It implies you don't trust him;
- No matter how weary and hungry you are after a long day in the saddle, always tend to your horse's needs before your own, and get your horse some feed before you eat;
- Do not practice ingratitude;
- A cowboy is pleasant even when out of sorts. Complaining is what quitters do, and cowboys hate quitters;
- Always be courageous. Cowards aren't tolerated in any outfit worth its salt;
- A cowboy always helps someone in need, even a stranger or an enemy;

- Be hospitable to strangers. Anyone who wanders in, including an enemy, is welcome at the dinner table. The same was true for riders who joined cowboys on the range;
- Give your enemy a fighting chance;
- Real cowboys are modest;
- Be there for a friend when he needs you;
- Drinking on duty is grounds for instant dismissal and blacklisting;
- A cowboy is loyal to his "brand," to his friends, and those he rides with;
- Never shoot an unarmed or unwarned enemy. This was also known as "the rattlesnake code": always warn before you strike. However, if a man was being stalked, this could be ignored;
- Never shoot a woman no matter what;
- Consideration for others is central to the code, such as: Don't stir up dust around the chuckwagon, don't wake up the wrong man for herd duty, etc.;
- Respect the land and the environment by not smoking in hazardous fire areas, disfiguring rocks, trees, or other natural areas;
- Honesty is absolute - your word is your bond, a handshake is more binding than a contract;
- Live by the Golden Rule.

Since the Code of the West was not a formal set of laws, any man who failed to abide by it was not formally punished. However, he would likely have been treated as a social outcast. We shall encounter several of these ideas again as they are expressed in one or more of the creeds and codes of the B western heroes.

The Code of the West found its way into the popular conscience mostly by way of entertainment, beginning with popular literature. Zane Grey, author of many Western novels and particularly one published in 1934, "The Code of the West," was arguably the first to popularize the standards listed above as well as some other standards for cowboy behavior. In his fictional stories, Grey based his characters upon the cowboy traditions and mythology that later spread to the movie industry, thus creating in the popular imagination ideas about the historical American West and its cowboys that still exist today. With the coming of television in the 1950s, Hollywood packaged the Code of the West along with the B western stars as part of its entertainment aimed at capturing the juvenile viewers in the new medium.

As we learn about these cowboy heroes and their creeds and codes, some modern readers may consider the entire idea of a Code of the West to be outdated, corny, or at best, nostalgic. However, some readers may find that the notion of a set of values that represent core principles of right and wrong resonates quite well with ordinary people who sense a lack of such standards being visible in today's culture.

Following the economic crisis of 2008, author Jim Owen wrote a book in which he applied the old Cowboy Codes to modern times in the context of business and social ethics. Owen wrote the book, titled "Cowboy Ethics: What Wall Street Can Learn from the Code of the West," out of his concern about the apparent lack of ethics among certain Wall Street business leaders and the general decline of ethics observed in modern society. In an interview with a newspaper reporter, Owen referred to the influence of the values exemplified by the early television cowboy heroes: "I grew up with Roy Rogers and Gene Autry, and they were my heroes. And today, my hero is the working cowboy. And it's that optimism, the courage, the hard work, that built the country. We've gotten away from these common-sense core values." Owen is therefore a representative of a group of people – perhaps a larger group than we might initially think – who readily see in the Code of the West a set of timeless values and virtues.

In today's world, a set of standard societal values to provide guidance in discerning between right and wrong is as necessary as it ever was. The fact that many people in the past and present failed to live up to such standards does not negate the value of having and teaching them. If we use the "life is a highway" metaphor, the presence of maps and road signs does not guarantee all travelers will drive properly or even reach their destination without getting lost; but at least they will have the right information – and many will find their way!

With this brief look into the history of the Code of the West now complete, we turn our attention to a survey of the early television B western heroes and their codes. In the chapters which follow, one will see that two characteristics are common to nearly all of the cowboy creeds that we will review, and are worth noting here at the beginning. First is that the creeds spoke to behavior that applies to all of us in every walk of life, not just for cowboys. Secondly, the creeds assume a Higher Power to which all –

including the cowboy heroes – are accountable for their actions and behavior. This assumption is explicit in some creeds, and at least implicit in all of them.

Our main focus will be on the codes and creeds of the "big 4" of 1950s television cowboy stars: Roy Rogers, Gene Autry, William "Hopalong Cassidy" Boyd, and the Lone Ranger. We then will take a more cursory look at several other cowboy heroes and their codes. Given that many modern readers may be unfamiliar with some of the stars discussed in these chapters, the information will be presented in a format intended to help acquaint the reader with that star's image, impact, and value as a role model. Thus, each hero will be introduced with an attempt to provide context for that hero and their code or creed: who he/she was as a cowboy hero; their impact on the culture; their code or creed; and observations regarding their impact as role models. When discussing each hero's published code or creed, two perspectives will be considered: the direct connection with teachings found in the Bible, and the connection between the code and their behavior observed in their television program's storylines.

Codes of the West

2

ROY ROGERS

OPENING CREDITS

On the television screen was seen a film clip with a close-up of each character in a fast-riding scene as the announcer spoke their name: "Post, the cereals you like the most, present ... *The Roy Rogers Show* starring Roy Rogers, King of the Cowboys ... Trigger, his golden Palomino ... and Dale Evans, Queen of the West ... With Pat Brady, his comical sidekick ... and Roy's Wonder Dog, Bullet."

"King of the Cowboys"

Roy Rogers was the King of the Cowboys, but he was the last of the "Big 4" to show up on network television when his show finally debuted at the end of 1951. William "Hopalong Cassidy" Boyd was the first, with some of his old Hopalong Cassidy movies airing on NBC in 1949, although his made-for-TV series did not begin until September, 1952. *The Lone Ranger* was the first of the "Big 4" to premiere with made-for-TV episodes, with the series starring Clayton Moore hitting the television airwaves in September, 1949. Then came Gene Autry with his filmed-for-TV series debut in July, 1950. Roy Rogers, who at the time was in the midst of a run of twelve consecutive years as the Number One Money-Making Western Star (according to the *Motion Picture Herald*), was still under contract to Republic. The movie studio wanted to avoid the risk of competition from television concerning their number one Western movie box-office draw. However, when Roy's contract with Republic ended May 27, 1951, Roy wasted no time in establishing a production company to begin filming *The Roy Rogers Show*.

The first of 100 episodes of *The Roy Rogers Show* aired on December 30, 1951, and the last first-run episode on June 9, 1957, all on Sunday evenings on NBC. New fans were continually attracted as the series continued in reruns on CBS and in syndication over a large number of stations from 1958 until 1964. With the series airing continually on so many stations for such an extended period of time, the show had the opportunity to influence the character development of an entire generation of viewers. In its third season on the air, *The Roy Rogers Show* was the number ten show in the Nielsen ratings for the 1953-1954 season, as noted in the July, 17, 1954 *TV Guide* article, "Why Roy Rogers Is Cowboy King." The article reported Roy, who also had a successful western adventure show on radio, was "now No. 1 in several different directions at once, all lucrative." During the 1954-1955 season, in which Roy's television show remained in the top-30 in the Nielsen ratings, readers of *TV-Radio Mirror* voted Roy as "Favorite TV Western Star" and his NBC TV show as "Favorite TV Western Program" (*TV-Radio Mirror*, May, 1955).

The popularity of Roy Rogers in film, radio, and television can be attributed to a combination of several factors. Roy was good-natured, could ride and handle a horse like he was born to do it, and had a well-known background in cowboy and western music as one of the founding members of the now-legendary Sons of the Pioneers (known for iconic songs like "Cool Water" and "Tumbling Tumbleweeds"). Just as important as any of those things was Roy's reputation as a man who in real life lived up to the ideals of his on-screen image, a fact that was noted in a May, 1954 article of *TV- Radio Mirror*: "Roy Rogers' real and radio lives are very much alike-and he loves them both." Roy's integrity and moral character were apparently well-known to colleagues even before he became a big star. "That is the true success story of Roy Rogers—and much more interesting than a listing of how many pictures he has made or how big a bank account he has," stated the author of "What Makes a Person Interesting," in the March, 1956 issue of *TV-Radio Mirror*. It is noteworthy that decades later, Roy and his wife Dale Evans, are the only western heroes included in a list of 50 heroes in the first edition of the book, *50 American Heroes Every Kid Should Meet*, by

Dennis Denenberg and Lorraine Roscoe.

The Roy Rogers Show enjoyed great success, if measured by the combination of the respectable ratings it achieved in its seven first-run years on NBC and its long life in reruns. By the end of March, 1959, the show was sponsored in syndication by Nestle and was being seen in 88 television markets – equal viewing coverage to some network shows (*Sponsor*, March 28, 1959). The continued exposure in syndication meant new generations of young viewers were constantly becoming fans of Roy.

Even before getting his show on television, Roy had built up an enormous fan base. Within three months of the 1949 founding of the Riders Club, membership was reported to be around 1,700,000 boys and girls, and 3,000 local chapters by 1950. This was in addition to the 2,000 Roy Rogers-Dale Evans fan clubs in the U.S. by 1950. Roy's fan club in London was reported to have 50,000 members, thought to be the largest fan club for any individual in the world at the time (Rinker, *Rinker on Collectibles*). All of these pre-TV fans of Roy's likely accounted for the large number of adults in the viewing audience for his television show, for which viewer demographics revealed that more adults were watching the show than children (White, *King of the Cowboys, Queen of the West*). By the late 1950s, the exposure to audiences through the TV show and to an estimated 100 million Americans in live performances and appearances had made Roy Rogers and Dale Evans household names throughout America. In addition to sending Roy a reported million fan letters per year, his many fans were a ready market for approximately four hundred Roy Rogers and Dale Evans products, including western boots, alarm clocks, rocking horses, comic books, lunch boxes, pajamas, and, of course, cap pistols.

The Roy Rogers Show was a thirty-minute western adventure show that was set in the mythical western area, Paradise Valley, but in a contemporary time setting that allowed for the regular use of amenities like electricity, telephones, and cars. The show featured three main characters: Roy Rogers, a prominent ranch owner; Dale Evans, owner of the Eureka Café in Mineral City; and Pat Brady, a cook at Dale's restaurant and foreman at Rogers' Double R Bar Ranch. To the added delight of millions of young viewers, the other regulars in the show were Trigger (Roy's famous horse), Buttermilk (Dale horse), and Roy's German Shepherd, Bullet.

One of the things that distinguished the show from the competition was the regular presence of a female, Dale, who was at times like a female

> "For more than half a century in the public spotlight, Roy Rogers represented decency, morality, and Christian values."
>
> (O'Neal, *American Cowboy*, undated.)

sidekick, and often, an independent-minded heroine. Though married in real life, Roy and Dale's relationship on screen was portrayed as one of good friends – not boyfriend and girlfriend. She owned and ran the Eureka Café and Hotel in Mineral City, in addition to owning and managing a small ranch. Though Roy was obviously the hero in the stories, Dale's character was spunky and independent, and more than a few times played a key role in apprehending the bad guys.

Roy and Dale worked as a team to solve the problem in each episode, with comic relief – and occasional help – provided by Pat Brady. Pat's character always wanted to be in the action, but tended to complicate things for Roy to the point that Dale would then be called upon to rescue Roy from a critical situation. Trigger was Roy's horse, faithful and smart, who could respond to Roy's cues for assistance in any situation. Bullet, Roy's "Wonder Dog," was a constant companion who could be relied upon to track bad guys and missing persons, carry messages, or summon help. Pat's jeep, "Nellybelle," was, in a sense, the final member of the show's cast. Nellybelle was mechanical, but to the everlasting frustration of Pat, the jeep seemed to have a mind of its own.

The typical story involved Roy coming upon someone in trouble – they have been robbed, threatened, falsely accused, ambushed, or were in some sort of desperate situation – or arriving at the invitation of some law enforcement officer seeking Roy's help. The central plot included the usual B Western themes such as bank robberies, cattle rustling, and mining, and also more contemporary themes like conservation of natural resources and gun safety. The story proceeded with plenty of action and adventure, plus some humor, and a healthy dose of values aimed at children. Often, the scripts included the expression of Christian themes, and it was common for Roy or Dale to conclude an episode with a statement or observation relating a moral principle. While most stories were built around the battle between good and evil, in many stories Roy and Dale would also point out the trouble one brings upon themselves when they fail to do the right thing. The stories are timeless in this sense, as Roy described in an interview for

TV-Radio Mirror in May, 1956: "The basic thing in drama, in history and in life is the conflict between good and evil. It goes on inside us all the time and it goes on outside us all the time."

As noted by author Raymond White, to the extent the scripts were a bit "preachy" at times, it did not seem to lower the show's ratings nor hurt the merchandising of Rogers-endorsed products (White, *King of the Cowboys, Queen of the West*). On screen, Roy – and Dale – expressed a concern for youth that came off as authentic, and was reinforced by their off-screen real-life actions and attitudes. An article in the July 17, 1954 issue of *TV Guide* explored the intangible bond that seemed to exist between the show's stars and their viewing audience – both children and their parents. The article noted Roy and his wife, Dale Evans, both love children and "there is no sham about this," as the couple was simply applying their basic philosophy, "to love children is to love God." In a May, 1956 issue of *TV-Radio Mirror*, Roy and Dale were again praised for being role models unspoiled by their commercial successes: "TWO FOR ALL . . . and everyone's for Roy and Dale, who reign as king and queen of the Golden Rule."

Public expressions of Christianity were a part of both *The Roy Rogers Show* and the personal lives of Roy and Dale. From a viewer's perspective, author Raymond White noted: "The emphasis on Christianity also set apart *The Roy Rogers Show* from its TV competitors, including, among others, *The Lone Ranger*, *The Gene Autry Show*, *Hopalong Cassidy*, *The Cisco Kid*, *Wild Bill Hickok*, *Annie Oakley*, and *Kit Carson*. All of these programs emphasized action and morality, but they did not overtly preach Christianity as did the Rogers series." (White, *King of the Cowboys, Queen of the West*).

Over the years, many articles appeared in newspapers and magazines reporting on the spiritual values evident in the daily lives of the Rogers family. For example, in an article in *TV-Radio Mirror*, the writer emphasized the widely reported fact that the Rogers family made spiritual development a priority: "Which brings us to a major point in the Rogers Family Plan . . . their spiritual upbringing of the children. Both feel it to be vital—the stabilizing background a child needs to draw upon in later life and even during schooldays, to combat deleterious influences. Both went to Sunday School as children, sang in the choir, and regularly attended church." (*TV-Radio Mirror*, June 1952).

This dual expression – in their fictional TV stories and in their real lives

– of solid values and good morals appealed to parents and other adults who frequently worked with children, and left an enduring impression on the lives of many people. At that time, even secular institutions were comfortable endorsing Roy, as seen, for example, in the early 1950s when *The Roy Rogers Show* was recommended for children's viewing by the Los Angeles District of Parent-Teachers Association. Today, many Christians still find Roy – and Dale – to be an inspiration for living out their Christian faith. It is perhaps the most meaningful part of Roy's legacy. John Riggs, a cowboy and preacher who was pastor of the 1200-member Bar None Cowboy Church near Tatum, Texas, was once quoted in an interview about the cowboy church movement: "The explosion of cowboy churches in recent years has roots in the open Christianity of the King of the Cowboys." (O'Neal, *American Cowboy*, retrieved January 12, 2015 from AmericanCowboy.com).

In 1949, almost three years before his television show began, Roy Rogers founded his Roy Rogers Riders Club for his young fans. Boys and girls across America mailed to Roy their name and address and then received a "Rogersgram" by "Trigger Express" containing several membership items. Their membership card to the club listed the Riders Club Rules. The principles contained in the rules were observed by Roy in his character's actions throughout the episodes of the TV series, and, as we will see, each of the rules had a sound basis in Biblical teaching.

Riders Club Rules and Creed

1. Be neat and clean.
2. Be courteous and polite.
3. Always obey your parents.
4. Protect the weak and help them.
5. Be brave, but never take chances.
6. Study hard, and learn all you can.
7. Be kind to animals and care for them.
8. Eat all your food and never waste any.
9. Love God and go to Sunday School regularly.
10. Always respect our flag and our country.

The Riders Club Rules and Creed were listed in detail on the back page of the *Official Roy Rogers Riders Club Comics* for the easy reference of club members. It was distinct from most other Western star's codes or creeds in its exposition provided with each of the rules, as will be seen below. The comic's back page displayed the short form of each rule, plus some additional commentary provided in more personal language – similar in tone and content to the *Hopalong Cassidy* episode trailers we will see later.

1.   Be neat and clean. At our house, Dale and I are pretty strict about Cheryl, Linda and Dusty keeping their rooms in neat order, putting away their toys when they've finished playing and hanging up their clothes. Remember, your mother is a busy person and just think of how much you can help if you keep your own things neat.

Some readers may be surprised to learn the Bible has a fair amount to say about this topic. In the Old Testament, the Israelites had clear instructions on how to maintain cleanliness in their homes and community. It was important enough that God instructed Moses to include these instructions as part of their law. There were recorded incidents where Moses was to specifically allow opportunities for the Israelites to wash their clothes (see Exodus 19:10). In Exodus 40:30-32, we see the provision of a basin with water to be used for washing of the hands and feet. Throughout the books of Leviticus and Deuteronomy, lengthy passages are devoted to the detailing of specific rules regarding cleanliness and sanitation. In the New Testament, the Jewish traditional washing of hands is mentioned in Mark 2. Later, Christians are taught our bodies are God's temple, and as such, we are responsible for proper care of our bodies (see I Corinthians 3:16-17, and I Corinthians 6:19-20). Thus, keeping one's things in neat order and clean is an important part of maintaining the level of personal hygiene and sanitation that is expected in scripture. Roy's comments added this behavior is also a way to honor one's parents – one of the Ten Commandments.

In the episodes of *The Roy Rogers Show*, what little we get to see of Roy's ranch home gives the impression that Roy kept a tidy house. However, the best example in the series of this creed article comes by way of Dale's high standards for maintaining a neat and clean operation at her Eureka Café. Pat Brady, who is employed at the café, is frequently seen sweeping the floor, wiping the counter, and generally helping keep the place clean for

Dale's customers. Whenever Pat is attempting to experiment with a new recipe or tinkering with new equipment, it usually has the comical outcome of creating a mess. Dale is then always quick to follow up by making sure Pat promptly cleans up his own mess – even if it means he will miss taking part in chasing the bad guys! There are also occasions in which Dale is observed assisting someone with their household chores.

The Rogers family in real life set a good example here, as well. It was reported in a 1952 magazine article that even though the family employed household helpers, "…the girls make their own beds and tidy their own rooms, wash out socks and do other small chores, as well as managing their allowances. Dale, who does the supermarketing for the household, takes all three along with her."

Maintaining a neat and clean home was thus included as a rule for members of the Riders Club. This was a valued behavior all Riders Club members could follow, regardless of economic status. For, as Roy, Pat, and Oley sang in the episode, "Outlaw's Return," "…*Be it ever so humble, there's no place like home.*"

2. Be courteous and polite. Saying "please" and "thank you" may not seem too important, but the boys and girls who always remember to be polite to their parents, teachers and friends are the ones I always feel make the best Riders Club members.

Treating one another in a kind manner is an application of the Golden Rule, spoken by Jesus and recorded in Matthew 7:12 (NLT) – "Do to others whatever you would like them to do to you. This is the essence of all that is taught in the law and the prophets." At the end of season four's episode, "Dead End Trail," Roy reminded everyone that the Golden Rule is the one primary rule that we all need to remember.

Numerous scriptures stress this behavior, such as Proverbs 18:21, which states that "death and life are in the power of the tongue" and Proverbs 16:24 (KJV): "Pleasant words are as an honeycomb, sweet to the soul, and health to the bones." Other New Testament verses speak of showing love one to another (e.g. John 13:35) and to excel at – or "outdo each other in" – showing honor to others (Romans 12:10). In the Old Testament, we read that the words of a virtuous woman are characterized by the law of kindness (Proverbs 31:26).

On one occasion, Jesus took it a step further when he told a crowd of people to "Love your enemies, bless them that curse you, do good to them that hate you, and pray for them which despitefully use you, and persecute you." (Matthew 5:44, KJV). This challenge to be courteous and polite in the context of how one treats their enemies was explored in the season four episode, "The Ginger Horse." In the story, Roy observes that the Bible in the young girl's home has been frequently opened to the Matthew 5:44 passage. The characters acknowledge the difficulty in living up to the standards set in that verse. At the close of the story, Roy plays the guitar as the group joins in singing "The Bible Tells Me So" – including the lyrics "*do good to your enemies…*"

Throughout the episodes of the series, Roy, Dale, and Pat consistently treated those with whom they came into contact – regardless of wealth, age, vocation, etc. – with courtesy and respect. In season five's episode, "Money Is Dangerous," viewers were reminded not to judge a person by outward appearances. In season four's "Born Fugitive," Dale tells a little girl that in Sunday School children learn "to love and to trust each other, and to do unto others as they would have others do unto them."

In the season five episode, "Bad Neighbors," the theme of treating each other with respect is again encountered. In the story, Roy works to bring about an agreement between feuding ranchers and farmers. Once accomplished, he states "there's always a peaceful way to settle an argument." Dale agrees, "Yes, if people would just take the time to find it." Roy concludes, "and they can find it if they're willing to see both sides of the problem."

Failing to extend common courtesy to strangers can have unintended consequences, as seen in season four's episode, "Strangers." Newcomers had arrived in Paradise Valley, but were not befriended by their neighbors. This then led to the newcomers becoming entangled with outlaws, whom they – in their loneliness – had mistaken for friendly neighbors. Roy pointed out the root of the problem in this case was the fact that "they came here as strangers and we let them stay that way." Dale then summed up: "Yes, and there's a lesson in that for us. If law-abiding people don't make friends with newcomers, the lawless will!" Pat heartily agreed, "You're right," and resolved that, "From now on, when I see a stranger I'm gonna walk right up to him and say, 'Howdy!'"

3. Always obey your parents. Sometimes you may think your parents are asking you to do something you feel isn't necessary or they may

refuse to let you have your own way. Believe me, pardners, your parents are just doing what they feel will be best for you - remember, they were young once too and maybe felt the same way you do.

It is implicit in the TV series that children are to honor and obey their parents — sometimes in circumstances where faith and trust on the part of the child is required in order to do so. The well-known verse in Colossians commands children to "obey your parents in all things: for this is well pleasing unto the Lord." (Colossians 3:20, KJV). Of course, honoring one's father and mother is also one of the Ten Commandments, recorded in Exodus 20:12 (KJV), and as Jesus noted, a commandment that comes with a promise ("that thy days may be long…"). Proverbs 13:1 (KJV) counsels the young with the advice that "a wise son heareth his father's instruction, but a scorner heareth not rebuke." In the episode, "Empty Saddles," Roy summarized the moral of that episode's story: "Well, no one can avoid trouble by running away from it — it always catches up with ya'. And when it does, it's worse than if you'd have faced it in the first place." It is therefore better to obey in the first place!

Perhaps even more interesting, though, is the observation that throughout the series, the parental role is more explicitly dealt with in the area of parent-child relationships. While children are commanded to obey their parents, the Bible also teaches the vital responsibilities parents have for their children. They are responsible for training their children how to live and behave (Proverbs 22:6, Deuteronomy 6), and failure to do so can bring shame upon the parents and child alike (Proverbs 19:15).

In season one's episode, "Badman's Brother," Roy and Dale help a father correct the behavior of his young son, Larry, who had gotten off to a bad start in life. At the end of the story, Dale states, "You know, saving Larry and boys and girls like him from making a wrong start is about one of the most important things that we grown-ups can do." This idea was repeated in a season two episode, "Hunting for Trouble." Roy observes that the outlaw in the story, Oley, had showed signs of having a good heart. With regards to Oley and his gang, Roy noted: "If they'd have been raised to respect and obey the law, they'd have probably grown up to be good men instead of outlaws."

Parent-child relationships were central to the story in the season six episode, "Johnny Rover," in which Mr. Revere, a wealthy, but tyrannical father, is exasperated by the estranged relationship he has with his son. Finally, in a conversation with Dale inside her Eureka Café, he asks, "What else could I have given him?"

Dale answers, "A little bit of yourself!"

Mr. Revere asks, "What do you mean?"

Dale then explains, "Look, Mr. Revere - out here in the West, we're used to seeing a boy grow up with his father. They do things together. They work together and play together – hunt, fish, ride!"

Thus, as Riders Club members contemplated the article to always obey their parents, several episodes reminded viewers that parents have a responsibility in this relationship, as well.

4. Protect the weak and help them. A true Riders Club member never tries to "bully" anyone, especially someone smaller or weaker than himself, instead he tries to do whatever he can to help them grow stronger.

The Bible has a lot to say about this Riders Club rule, and in essence, this is what all the B western heroes were about – coming to the aid of the weak and oppressed. In the Old Testament, we find commands forbidding the oppression of the poor and needy, including strangers (Deuteronomy 24:14), and expressly forbidding oppressing – "bullying" – each other (Leviticus 25:17). Proverbs 3:31 also warns against choosing the ways of the oppressor. Rather, the Bible instructs us to help the weaker, more vulnerable members of society. In Isaiah 1:17 (NLT), the Israelites were told, "Learn to do good. Seek justice. Help the oppressed. Defend the cause of orphans. Fight for the rights of widows." Also, in Psalm 82:3 (KJV), we see the command to, "defend the poor and fatherless: do justice to the afflicted and needy." These same behaviors are commanded and commended in numerous scriptures throughout the Old and New Testaments.

In the TV series, every episode presented Roy and his friends coming to the aid of those in need. More often than not, they were helping the oppressed, orphans, widows, and so on. In the season two episode, "The Long Chance," the outlaws thought of their lifestyle as fun and adventurous, giving little or no regard to the reality they were hurting others. As the story was building to its climax, the following dialogue occurred.

GRUNDY (the outlaw leader in the episode): You've got this robbery business all wrong. You know it isn't just the money that counts — it's a, it's kind of a game.

PAT BRADY: What kind of a game? I thought I knew 'em all!

GRUNDY: See if a man puts his money in the bank or a safe, he's just practically darin' me to try and get it! Shucks if he was to leave it in the open, listen, it wouldn't be any fun. You know, Roy, if you was to throw in with me, we could really do big things!

PAT: Don't you listen to him, Roy. He's just tryin' to tempt you down the road of sin!

GRUNDY: What's sinful about it? It's a swell life! Livin' in the open keeps ya healthy, ya get to see a lot of the country and ya got plenty of money to spend!

ROY: Yeah? Where? You can't even go to a decent restaurant. You can't live in a decent home. Can't even own your own horse for fear somebody'll recognize it. All stolen money'll buy is hate and greed — even from your own men!

Roy's message was clear. In the end, a life spent oppressing others would not end well, and it was folly to think otherwise. A Riders Club member must therefore follow the lead of Roy in the defending of the weak and a willingness to help those in need. In real life, as noted earlier, Roy and Dale were effective role models for their fans in this regard.

5. Be brave, but never take chances. Just remember the fellow who takes a "dare" isn't always the "hero." Bravery means doing whatever you can to help someone in trouble, but not taking reckless chances where you yourself might get hurt.

In the season one episode, "Dead Man's Hills," Pat Brady states he does not think it would be a wise move to make a direct rush at the outlaws who are hiding out in a mine entrance. Roy agrees, "Well, risking lives isn't the sheriff's idea of a good law man." Pat responds, "Yeah, him and me both!" Pat was effectively echoing the thoughts found in verses like Proverbs 3:21-23, which speak of using sound wisdom and discretion to maintain personal safety, and Exodus 23:13, which speaks of being "circumspect" (aware of one's circumstances).

Taking unnecessary chances is clearly frowned upon in scripture.

Anyone who has seen a lot of television westerns has frequently witnessed a scene wherein an individual is pressured into accepting a dare and doing something illegal or unethical to avoid the dreaded label of "being yellow" or "scared." Jesus' famous time of facing temptation in the wilderness (see Matthew 4) involved Jesus successfully resisting three "dares" to gain supposed glory by engaging in very risky behavior. In Proverbs 1:10 (KJV), we are warned, "if sinners entice thee, consent thou not." Elsewhere throughout Proverbs we see advice like "discretion shall preserve thee" (2:11), and "a prudent man foreseeth the evil, and hideth himself; but the simple pass on, and are punished" (22:3), and again, "the prudent man looketh well to his going" (14:15). In general, one's behavior should always be such that it pleases God, according to scripture. In Galatians 1:10 (KJV), the test of our motives and actions is given by posing the questions, "do I now persuade men, or God? Or do I seek to please men?" The answer matters, according to I Samuel 2:3 (KJV), where we read that "the Lord is a God of knowledge, and by Him actions are weighed."

Taking unnecessary risks should be avoided even in supposedly harmless activities like gambling, according to Roy in the season six episode, "Fishing for Fingerprints," in which he quotes Mark Twain: "There are two times in a man's life when he shouldn't gamble – one is when he can't afford it, the other is when he can."

Being brave, but not reckless, stresses the issue of safety, as well. In the season six episode, "Junior Outlaw," Roy and Dale had the opportunity to address the importance of teenagers following the rules for safe driving. As the young driver got behind the wheel to take some friends for a drive in his first car, Roy lectured him: "It isn't how fast, but how safely you drive. You know a car can be just as dangerous as a gun if it isn't used properly." Dale agreed: "That's right. More people are hurt by speed and disregard of the other drivers' rights than by any other cause." Pat Brady added: "Always be courteous and drive careful and go easy on that gas pedal and you'll stay outta trouble!"

Perhaps this part of Roy's creed can be nicely summed up in Roy's advice to Elmer Kirby, the photographer in season one's episode, "Shoot to Kill," at the end of that story: "You know, tryin' to be what we're not sometimes gets us into a lot of trouble."

6.   Study hard and learn all you can. Everyone has a job to do all his life, and when you're young, school is your "office" and your lessons

are your "work." And, the work you do in school pays off with the best jobs when you grow older.

Many things change over time, but one thing that seems to remain the same from generation to generation is the preference of students to avoid the classroom! It is the rare child who enjoys having their "nose stuck in a book" more than running around the playground. Among those who enjoy reading, most would prefer to choose their own reading material rather than laboring through assigned reading. However, the Bible clearly states the importance of gaining knowledge and wisdom through study. There are several characters in the Bible who could serve as "poster boys" for obtaining a formal education, among them Moses, Daniel, Luke, and Paul. Consider also the following scriptures:

Proverbs 16:16 (KJV): "How much better is it to get wisdom than gold! And to get understanding rather to be chosen than silver!"

Ecclesiastes 9:16a, 18a (KJV): "Then said I, Wisdom is better than strength. Wisdom is better than weapons of war."

Ecclesiastes 7:12b (KJV): "Wisdom giveth life to them that have it."

Isaiah 33:6a (KJV): "And wisdom and knowledge shall be the stability of thy times."

Proverbs 8:33 (KJV): "Hear instruction, and be wise, and refuse it not."

Proverbs 18:15 (KJV): "The heart of the prudent getteth knowledge; and the ear of the wise seeketh knowledge."

Proverbs 19:20 (KJV): "Hear counsel, and receive instruction, that thou mayest be wise in thy latter end."

In the season six episode, "Accessory to Crime," a father is working hard to save money and finance his son's way through college. He soon learns his son recognizes the importance of obtaining a college education and has been working hard to earn money to help pay his own way through college. Perhaps the boy had read Proverbs 4:5-6 (NLT), "Get wisdom; develop good judgment. Don't forget my words or turn away from them. Don't turn your back on wisdom, for she will protect you. Love her, and she will guard you."

In one story, Roy instructs a group of young boys that it is a healthy thing to be curious and desiring to learn, and that they should always feel free to ask questions. "If you run into anything you don't understand, don't be afraid to ask questions. That's what grown-ups are for, is to answer questions and help you kids," Roy assured the boys. In Deuteronomy 32:7 (NLT), Moses said it this way: "Remember the days of long ago; think about the generations past. Ask your father, and he will inform you. Inquire of your elders, and they will tell you."

Learning some things requires work and practice, as Pat Brady determined in "The Knockout," when he announced he was going to train to become a champ at boxing. Roy encouraged him – and the viewers – with his response: "You know we can all be champions at something if we just keep at it and don't throw in the sponge." We may make mistakes along the way, but as Roy once counseled a young man in a season two story ("Go for Your Guns"), "Everybody makes mistakes, Bob. It's the smart ones that profit by 'em." The key appears to be having a willingness to listen and persevere. In Proverbs 15:31 (NLT), we read "If you listen to constructive criticism, you will be at home among the wise."

Education can be acquired by both formal and informal means, and Roy's creed taught Riders Club members it would require applying one's self with a desire to listen, observe, and work – but was worth the effort required.

7. Be kind to animals and care for them. No matter what kind of a pet you have, always be sure to take good care of it, because that animal looks to you for protection and love. Animals are man's best friends and to keep our friends we have to show them how much we care for them.

Every fan of *The Roy Rogers Show* knew about Trigger, Dale's horse, Buttermilk, and Roy's Wonder Dog, Bullet. Roy admitted that many of his young fans who came to see him in his personal appearances were just as excited – often more excited – to meet Trigger! With the ever-present Trigger, Buttermilk, and Bullet (Roy and Dale's personal pet), Roy had full credibility with the Riders Club members on this rule.

While many are aware of the emphasis in the Bible of the value placed by God upon human life, some may be surprised to learn there are also passages of scripture that deal specifically with our responsibility for the proper care of animals. This was the case from the beginning, as we read in Genesis 1:26. Earlier in Genesis chapter 1, we are told that God created all the creatures of the animal kingdom, then in verse 26, we learn that man was to have dominion – or responsible oversight – over the animals God had created. Later in the Old Testament we read that "a righteous man regardeth the life of his beast" (Proverbs 12:10). It is part of the Bible's overall teaching of respect for life and accepting personal responsibility. Again, with the instruction seen in Proverbs 27:23 (ESV), we are taught that proper care for one's animals is expected: "Know well the condition of your flocks, and pay attention to your herds." In the Old Testament, proper care of animals extended to showing concern for your neighbor's animals, as well: "If you see your neighbor's ox or sheep or goat wandering away, don't ignore your responsibility. Take it back to its owner" (Deuteronomy 22:1, NLT).

Two episodes, in particular, had storylines that reinforced this Riders Club rule. In "Bullets and a Burro," an old prospector, named Scotty, has a beloved mule he calls Jewell. He thinks of Jewell as a treasured pet and friend, and at the end of the story, Scotty uses the proceeds from his prospecting efforts to purchase a piece of property and establish a haven for mules. In another story, "Horse Crazy," an outlaw was convinced his prize horse could outrun any other horse – including that in any posse. But while fleeing from the law, he loses a race to Roy's horse, Trigger. When the outlaw (named Judd) is quite saddened by the fact that his horse lost the race with Trigger, Roy explains, "He lost because you *made* him run. Trigger *wanted* to – he's my friend. He ran with his heart as well as his legs. You can't get the best out of a horse or a man by driving him. That's where you made your mistake, Judd!"

In real life, Riders Club members were likely well aware that Trigger, Buttermilk, and Bullet were personally owned by Roy Rogers and his family considering that national publications frequently mentioned such in their stories on Roy. According to such articles, Roy and Dale kept quite a few animals on their ranch for the pleasure of their family and the character-building of their kids. In a 1952 story in *TV Radio Mirror*, it was noted "Responsibility for the care of an animal or two, Roy feels, is something every child ought to learn."

8. Eat all your food and never waste any. Boys and girls in this country are the luckiest in the world. We have so many hundreds of foods to choose from that we can have anything we want to eat. Thousands of youngsters in Asia and Europe hardly have anything to eat and often have to go hungry. So, never waste any of your food, and then

America will have food to share with the less fortunate in other countries.

It is true that throughout Europe and Asia in the 1950s, thousands – if not millions – of children were living in poverty conditions brought about by so much destruction during World War Two in their homelands. Riders Club members were to be grateful for the abundance they could enjoy in the United States, showing their gratitude in part by eating the food provided by their parents, and being willing to share excess amounts with others. Jesus taught the virtues of providing food for the hungry in Matthew 25:35, and Paul, in Romans 12:13 taught Christians they should practice hospitality. Actions speak louder than words, according to the old axiom – and according to James 2:15-16 (ESV), which poses the question: "If a brother or sister is poorly clothed and lacking in daily food, and one of you says to them, 'Go in peace, be warmed and filled,' without giving them the things needed for the body, what good is that?"

In *The Roy Rogers Show*, Dale's Eureke Café was known by the folks in and around Mineral City for its fine food and good coffee. Pat Brady worked for Dale in the café, and was known to try new recipes and experiment with new cooking ideas – usually ending up with nothing more than a mess. However, Dale ran an efficient restaurant and was generous with her resources to share food or her guest room with those in need, including strangers.

In the season four episode, "Backfire," two children, Johnny and Debra, are shown to be in the habit of waiting for the giving of thanks before eating their food. When a guest (an outlaw posing as a minister) suggests the children be the ones to say grace at the table, Johnny begins, "The earth is the Lord's, and the fullness thereof." Debra, his sister, continues with, "And for this gift of food may we be truly thankful." All then conclude by saying in unison, "Amen."

9. Love God and go to Sunday School regularly. I hope all my Riders Club members go to Sunday School regularly, just like our own children do. Cheryl, Linda and Dusty know that going to church in the morning is the most important part of every Sunday.

Roy and Dale made no secret of the fact that they were church-attending Christians, and were raising their children accordingly. In fact, one could make the point that this well-known aspect of their lives lent all the more authenticity – and authority – to the "moralizing" found in the stories of their TV series and the rules for the Riders Club members. Magazine articles, like the one in the August, 1949 issue of *Radio and Television Mirror*, documented the family's habit of regularly attending both morning and evening services at their home church.

At the end of the season two episode, "The Feud," Roy and Dale are seen attending a wedding. During the ceremony, as the minister is speaking the words, "Dearly beloved, we are gathered together here in the sight of God to join together...", Dale echoes the phrase in a whisper to Roy, "In the sight of God ...", to which Roy softly responds: "That's where we always are; trouble is there's a lot of folks like Lee Harris and Ben Pierce [the two bad guys in this episode] that keeps forgetting that never for a moment are we out of the sight of the good Lord." To love God – the first part of this Riders Club rule – begins with a recognition that God exists and is always present.

Jesus' words in Matthew 22:37-38 (ESV) give us the command to "love the Lord your God with all your heart and with all your soul and with all your mind. This is the great and first commandment." I John 5:3 and other scriptures tell us that to love God is to keep His commandments. The writer of Ecclesiastes 12:13 (KJV) stated it as the primary goal of man: "Let us hear the conclusion of the whole matter: Fear [as in, love and respect] God, and keep His commandments: for this is the whole duty of man." The Bible contains the commandments of God by which we are expected to live, and "his commandments are not burdensome," according to I John 5:3 (ESV).

Roy gave spiritual advice to a prisoner at the end of the story in the season four episode, "Backfire," when the outlaw, Hook, is shown in his jail cell with a Bible in hand. While in jail, Hook had begun to get familiar with the location of various books in the Bible, and proudly demonstrated to Roy that he knew how to quickly navigate to Exodus, Psalms, and Romans. He eagerly asked Roy, "Ain't that somethin'?"

Roy responded, "Yes, but that book wasn't written to do tricks with – it was written to be read and lived by!"

Hook answered: "But I been readin' it! That's why I was wonderin', Mr. Rogers, if maybe I couldn't have this book?"

Roy assured him, "I think the Parson would want you to have it. And you can't own a better book!"

In another season four episode, "Hidden Treasure," the Bible is referred to as a book containing the key to the world's greatest treasure.

In the New Testament book of Hebrews, early Christians were urged to maintain a habit of regularly meeting together for worship and fellowship, and in the Old Testament, the Psalmist said, "One thing have I desired of the Lord, that will I seek after; that I may dwell in the house of the Lord all the days of my life, to behold the beauty of the Lord, and to inquire in His temple." (Psalm 27:4, KJV).

Roy and Dale – both in real life and in character – encouraged others to attend Sunday School and church, not from a sense of duty, but because there were tangible benefits. After the Sunday service had concluded in "Hidden Treasure," Parson Lode Turner stated, "You know, they ain't nothin' more edifyin' than a good sermon."

"There certainly isn't," agreed Dale.

"Puts ya' right with the world the rest of the week!", added Roy.

In another episode, "Born Fugitive," a little girl named Johnnie has never attended Sunday School and is frightened at the thought of going. However, Dale calms her and assures her "There's nothing to be afraid of – Sunday School is a wonderful place. That's where they teach children to live as God wants them to; where they teach them to love and to trust each other, and to do unto others as they would have others do unto them." Furthermore, Dale points out to Johnnie at the end of the story, "by going to church and learning about God, you'll learn to put all your problems in His hands and then it will be easy for you to distinguish between right and wrong. Johnnie, here you'll grow up with love!"

10. Always respect our flag and our country. We live in the greatest country in the world and it's up to all of us to do everything we can to show our love for America. Doing all we can to protect our freedom by following the laws of our country is one of the best ways in which we can show our love and respect.

This was a common theme among all of the early TV B Western heroes, and Roy was no exception. Victory in World War Two was not yet ten years in the past and patriotism was still at a high level. Pride in America and civic responsibility were common themes in both popular culture and the curriculum used in school systems across the country.

While the Bible does not endorse one form of government as superior to another, it does teach that God expects all people to be subject to their governing authorities. In Romans 13:1-7, we read that God is the ultimate authority and, thus, existing governments are those which, for whatever divine purpose, have been allowed or appointed by God. In verse 7, Christians are instructed to pay "taxes to whom taxes are owed, revenue to whom revenue is owed, respect to whom respect is owed, honor to whom honor is owed." (Romans 13:7, ESV). In the second letter from Peter, Christians were reminded to "honor the emperor" (I Peter 2:17, ESV), and in Titus 3:1 (ESV), a proactive involvement was expected: "Remind them to be submissive to rulers and authorities, to be obedient, to be ready for every good work."

In general, some variation on the theme of showing respect for the laws of the nation and local community was present in every episode of *The Roy Rogers Show*. To have a community of law-abiding citizens, a healthy respect for the law of the land is best accomplished when such is taught early in life. In the episode, "Smoking Guns," the responsibility for instilling the values corresponding to civic responsibility is presented as a joint venture between parents and civic leaders. At the end of the story, the chief of a local tribe makes a statement to that effect, to which Dale responds: "You're right, Chief. Keeping our young people on the right path is more important than gold."

In another episode, "Boys Day in Paradise Valley," the story centers around the opportunity given to several young boys in the town to serve in various local law-enforcement offices as part of "Boys Day." Roy, who was involved as a mentor to the boys that day, said it was a chance for the boys to learn more about citizenship.

Respecting the rights and privileges of our fellow citizens was the theme in a late-series episode titled, "Mountain Pirates." The story dealt with the responsible use of our natural resources in the context of recreational activities. At the end of the episode, Roy makes the statement: "When you disregard any of the rules of the forest - being careless with fires or disobey the rules of the fish and game commission - you're robbing every man, woman and child who love the great outdoors of their rightful pleasure." It is thus another way for Riders Club members to "show our love for America."

Role Models

In retrospect, what made Roy Rogers and Dale Evans stand out so much was their living out their faith, including the tenets expressed in the Riders Club Rules, in a consistent manner through good and bad times. Their visibility to the public – combined with Dale's writing – made it easy for everyone to know what they stood for, and to see how Roy and Dale consciously lived their lives by aspiring to those same high standards. Roy and Dale knew they were held up as role models for the youth in America, and continually strove to earn and maintain the viewers' trust. It is as though their real life was being described in the dialogue ending the episode, "Hard Luck Story," when Roy told Pat Brady "A man can't rest on the reputation he's made, Pat. He has to keep on makin' it every day of his life." To this, Dale added: "Roy's right. A reputation is just like wallpaper – it can be pasted on, but it has to have something solid underneath to make it stick!"

In their autobiography, Roy later wrote on the subject of being role models:

We were put in a position to be role models for many American boys and girls, and believe me, we have taken that job seriously. We have always been careful to act the way we feel children ought to see their heroes behave on screen as well as off. In our TV show, we made Dale's place the Eureka Café, not some saloon where drinks were served. And even off-camera, we've tried to portray a good image. ... I've always told my kids that their image is important. That's what you've got in life: your handshake and the image you portray. When I'm talking about my image, I don't mean there's anything about it that isn't really me. It's just that I always try to be the best I can. I believe children should have heroes, not antiheroes. I think they need people to look up to. (Rogers and Evans, *Happy Trails: Our Life Story*).

Roy is fondly remembered by millions of fans today, and it seems fitting that he is remembered as much or more for what he stood for than for the actual stories in his films and TV series. Shortly after Roy passed away, the writer of an article in *American Cowboy* summed up Roy's legacy as follows:

For a while there, the man in the white hat on the golden palomino righted wrongs, rescued the weak, and reminded us all of why we're here. In his films and in the messages he's given us, though they may seem innocent and simplistic to modern audiences, he left behind a legacy. The code of conduct he prescribed for boys and girls was just one example. Good advice for little cowboys and cowgirls. Or big ones. Or the whole human race, for that matter. (Mullins, *American Cowboy*, Sept/Oct 1998).

As we have seen in the discussion of Roy's Riders Club Rules, various episodes expressed thoughts that were overtly Christian in nature. Roy and Dale were known to be honestly outspoken about the role their Christian faith played in their lives. It is not only what defined them in real life, but even during the years of their TV series in the 1950s, it distinguished them from other Western performers. Interestingly, especially in the context of today's entertainment culture in America, "the use of Christianity did not limit their professional or commercial achievements." (White, *King of the Cowboys, Queen of the West*).

As we continue with our review of the creeds and codes of other Western heroes, the overt connection to Christianity in their TV episodes will be much less prevalent, but still observable. We will see that the values expressed in their creeds and codes nicely align with Biblical teachings.

Bobby J. Copeland, author of more than a dozen books on the B Western heroes and more than 150 published articles on cowboys and their movies, commented on Roy Rogers as a role model:

"To me, he was father figure, pastor, Sunday School teacher, hero – all rolled into one." Of Roy's off-screen work, Copeland noted: "Roy never passed up an opportunity to do good work. He visited children's hospitals whenever he could, he gave money to lots of charities; he didn't like to talk about it though, he just did these things. He was very concerned about being a good model for kids."

– *Bobby J. Copeland*, as quoted in Martin Grams, Jr.'s blog of March 29, 2013.

Roy Rogers and Trigger in a promotional photo.

Front cover of the comic book included with the material for members of the Roy Rogers Riders Club.

Riders Club Rules and Creed

1. BE NEAT AND CLEAN.

At our house Dale and I are pretty strict about Cheryl, Linda and Dusty keeping their rooms in neat order, putting away their toys when they've finished playing and hanging up their clothes. Remember, your mother is a busy person and just think of how much you can help if you keep your own things neat.

2. BE COURTEOUS AND POLITE.

Saying "please" and "thank you" may not seem too important, but the boys and girls who always remember to be polite to their parents, teachers and friends are the ones I always feel make the best Riders Club members.

3. ALWAYS OBEY YOUR PARENTS.

Sometimes you might think your parents are asking you to do something you feel isn't necessary or they may refuse to let you have your own way. Believe me, pardners, your parents are just doing what they feel will be best for you—remember, they were young once too and maybe felt the same way you do.

4. PROTECT THE WEAK AND HELP THEM.

A true Riders Club member never tries to "bully" anyone, especially someone smaller or weaker than himself. Instead he tries to do whatever he can to help them grow stronger.

5. BE BRAVE BUT NEVER TAKE CHANCES.

Just remember the fellow who takes a "dare" isn't always the "hero." Bravery means doing whatever you can to help someone in trouble, but not taking reckless chances where you yourself might get hurt.

6. STUDY HARD AND LEARN ALL YOU CAN.

Everyone has a job to do all his life, and when you're young, school is your "office" and your lessons are your "work." And, the work you do in school pays off with the best jobs when you grow older.

7. BE KIND TO ANIMALS AND CARE FOR THEM.

No matter what kind of a pet you have, always be sure to take good care of it, because that animal looks to you for protection and love. Animals are man's best friends and to keep our friends we have to show them how much we care for them.

8. EAT ALL YOUR FOOD AND NEVER WASTE ANY.

Boys and girls in this country are the luckiest in the world. We have so many hundreds of foods to choose from that we can have anything we want to eat. Thousands of youngsters in Asia and Europe hardly have anything to eat and often have to go hungry. So, never waste any of your food, and then America will have food to share with the less fortunate in other countries.

9. LOVE GOD AND GO TO SUNDAY SCHOOL REGULARLY.

I hope all my Riders Club members go to Sunday School regularly, just like our own children do. Cheryl, Linda and Dusty know that going to church in the morning is the most important part of every Sunday.

10. ALWAYS RESPECT OUR FLAG AND OUR COUNTRY.

We live in the greatest country in the world and it's up to all of us to do everything we can to show our love for America. Doing all we can to protect our freedom by following the laws of our country is one of the best ways in which we can show our love and respect.

The back cover of the Official Roy Rogers Riders Club Comics book, showing the full version of the Riders Club rules.

THIS
CERTIFIES THAT

IS A MEMBER IN GOOD STANDING THE

ROY ROGERS RIDERS CLUB

AND IS EXPECTED TO FOLLOW The RULES FAITHF

Roy Rogers

KING OF THE COWBOYS

ROY ROGERS RIDERS RULES

1. Be neat and clean.
2. Be courteous and polite.
3. Always obey your parents.
4. Protect the weak and help them.
5. Be brave but never take chances.
6. Study hard and learn all you can.
7. Be kind to animals and care for them.
8. Eat all your food and never waste any.
9. Love God and go to Sunday School regularly.
10. Always respect our flag and our country.

Many Happy Trails *Roy Rogers & Trigger*

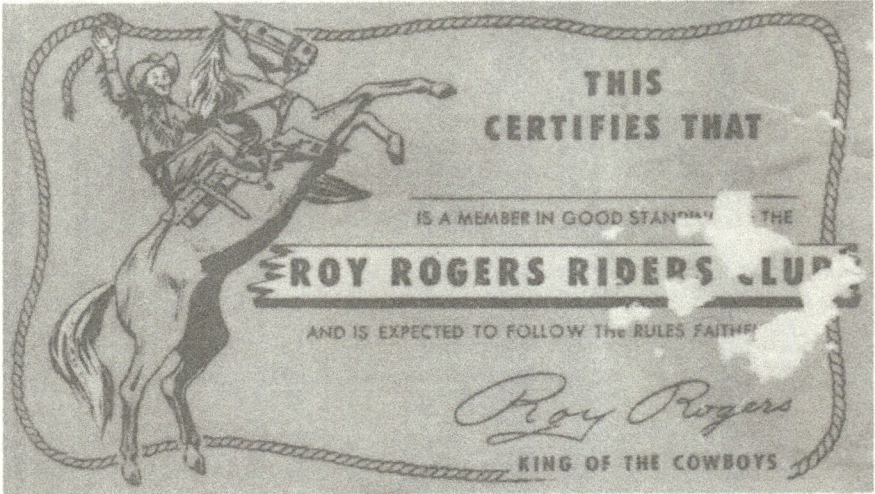

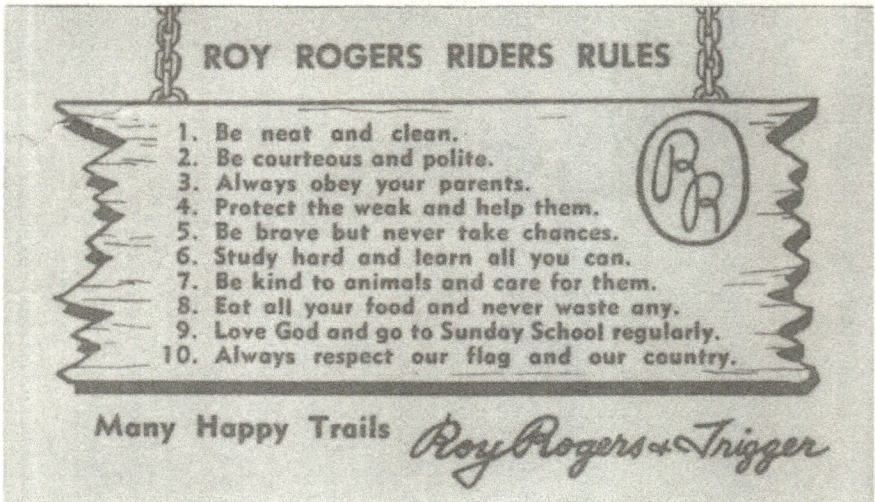

Front and back views of the membership card for the Riders Club.

This is a screenshot from a promotional trailer produced and paid for by Roy Rogers. It was distributed free to theater owners as a promotional incentive inviting kids to join the Riders Club.

3

GENE AUTRY

OPENING CREDITS

In the background could be heard Gene Autry singing "Back in the Saddle Again," while Gene's voice spoke a greeting: "Hello, folks. Say, I've got a swell story I wanna tell you today. Champ and I are ready for action." Then a narrator announced: "The Wriggly Company presents Gene Autry – America's Favorite Cowboy! And his horse, Champion – the World's Wonder Horse!"

"America's Favorite Cowboy"

Generally regarded as America's first superstar "singing cowboy," Gene Autry had an incredibly successful career as an entertainer, during which he also displayed a flair for success in a variety of business enterprises. His television series aired on CBS for five years on Sunday nights at 7:00 P.M., beginning in July, 1950. At the same time he was filming his TV series, he continued to star in his own weekly, western adventure radio show, filmed movies, released musical recordings, and oversaw the operations of his Flying A Pictures film company. Gene is the only individual to be awarded stars in all five performance categories on the Hollywood Walk of Fame.

Gene was the number one box office cowboy movie star when he left film-making to serve in the Army during World War Two. His initial duties included recruiting, entertaining the troops, and selling war bonds.

However, after earning his pilot's wings, he served in the Air Ferry Command where he co-piloted huge cargo planes of men and equipment to such far-flung theaters-of-war as India, China, and Burma. After the war, Gene returned to making movies and starring in his radio show, *Melody Ranch*, which was broadcast on Saturday evenings at 8:00 P.M. on the CBS radio network.

Ever the astute business man, Gene was quick to see the potential in the new medium of television and was already showing an interest in expanding to TV in January, 1948. When edited versions of Hopalong Cassidy films appeared on television in mid-1949, followed by the September, 1949 transition to television by *The Lone Ranger*, Gene wasted no time in getting his own made-for-TV films ready. Like Roy Rogers, Gene initially faced opposition from his movie studio – and movie theater chains – in his plans to enter television. However, Gene stuck with his intuition, realizing that television would open up a venue for exposure to new audiences who had not yet seen him. He gave a full explanation of his reasoning in an interview for *TV-Radio Mirror*:

> Now there are older people who see me on television who never before went to my pictures in theatres. They are learning that Westerns are exciting entertainment. Parents who got into the habit of watching with their children now tune in for themselves even when the youngsters are busy with their homework or have gone off to bed. Shut-ins who never got to theatres, hospital patients, and the littlest children who were too small to sit quietly in theatres, have all become part of the new audience. Some of these will eventually become theatre patrons, as a result of liking me on TV. It has given me a whole new group of fans. (*TV-Radio Mirror*, April, 1954).

Gene's television series began airing on Sunday, July 23, 1950, over the CBS network, and thus Gene arrived early on the television scene, with the Lone Ranger and the Cisco Kid being the only western heroes to precede him with specially made-for-TV half-hour films (*Sponsor*, September, 25, 1950). The series starred Gene and his sidekick, Pat Buttram, and ran until 1955, ending with ninety-one episodes.

TIME magazine's July 31, 1950 issue heralded Gene's arrival to television: "For the first time, an outstanding Hollywood star has made a movie designed especially for television. Cowboy Hero Gene Autry, second most popular western actor in the U.S., has finished six half-hour westerns for weekly release on CBS-TV. He plans to chain-produce at least 20 more in the next year." The article reported that while the show offered nothing new in its stories or characters, it was truly innovative in that: "The westerns that TV has been showing were made originally for movie theaters. Autry and his associates, in designing films for the smaller television screen, have made some long-needed technical changes." Long-shots were more or less eliminated, closer photography was used in riding scenes, and brighter lighting of scenes was used, with the use of more grey shades in color blends to avoid too much black on TV screens. All of these were cited as examples of the improvements in production values accomplished by Autry's team, contributing to a vastly improved viewing experience in television's early days. The final thirteen episodes of the series were filmed in color, although extremely few color TV sets were in use at the time they were originally broadcast in 1955.

The show was an immediate success story on television. The primary sponsor was Wrigley, the chewing gum company, but other sponsors were quick to cash in however they could, as well. For example, Gimbels in New York, which had a Gene Autry department in their store at the time, ran a tie-in contest for three weeks to help promote the show. Prizes included a trip to Hollywood with the winning child's parents, and a screen test by Autry's TV film company. (*Sponsor*, Sept 25, 1950). Gene received large amounts of fan mail, and even Champion, Autry's famed horse, was reported to be receiving a thousand pieces of fan mail per month in 1951. (*TV-Radio Mirror*, December, 1951). For the 1953-1954 season, Gene was voted by *TV-Radio Mirror* readers as Favorite TV Western Star and his show the Favorite TV Western Show. (*TV-Radio Mirror*, May, 1954).

The Gene Autry Show was a half-hour filmed western adventure series that starred Gene Autry and his television sidekick, Pat Buttram, in what was essentially a nicely produced thirty-minute version of Gene's B-Western movies. Music was an integral piece of the television series, with Gene performing at least one song in every episode – sometimes three or four songs in the same episode. Roy Rogers only rarely sang on his television show, leaving Gene as effectively the only "singing cowboy" on television.

In the stories throughout the series, Gene is seen in a variety of character roles – though always using the name Gene Autry – and places, rather than being based in any one locale. Pat always used the name Pat

Buttram, although in several stories, he and Gene were portrayed as strangers at the beginning of an episode. In some episodes, Gene was cast as a sheriff, a marshall, or perhaps an undercover government agent. In others, he was a ranch hand battling crooked cattlemen, or a local citizen helping endangered neighbors. On still other occasions, he and Pat themselves were the target of some evil doer and had to defend themselves. Some stories were set in the Old West of the 1800s, while a few were set in more modern times. Gene stated his goal with the TV show was simply to "get the best story we possibly can, cast it the best way we can, keep it clean, and do the best job of acting that we can." (*TV-Radio Mirror*, April 1954). Pat Buttram was a key part of the show with his ability to combine good acting with genuine western comedy ability.

In 1956, as *The Gene Autry Show* was being syndicated in reruns throughout the country, a reporter for *TV-Radio Mirror* speculated on the reason for the continuing popularity of Gene: "What is there about Gene Autry that wears so well? The answer is to be found in Gene's sincerity, his honesty of heart and manner, simple as one of his Western tunes. Plain folks, it seems, never wear out their welcome. And Gene Autry, with his simplicity, is forever welcome in his listeners' homes."

Cowboy Code of Honor

1. The Cowboy must never shoot first, hit a smaller man, or take unfair advantage.
2. He must never go back on his word, or a trust confided in him.
3. He must always tell the truth.
4. He must be gentle with children, the elderly, and animals.
5. He must not advocate or possess racially or religiously intolerant ideas.
6. He must help people in distress.
7. He must be a good worker.
8. He must keep himself clean in thought, speech, action, and personal habits.
9. He must respect women, parents, and his nation's laws.
10. The Cowboy is a patriot.

Gene Autry's cowboy code preceded the appearance of his show on television by a couple of years, appearing in print by around 1948. The code was apparently developed over a period of time, and was based on the same philosophies that guided the storylines in his *Melody Ranch* radio show and his movies.

Compared to *The Roy Rogers Show*, the dialogue in *The Gene Autry Show* was almost completely secular, with only a rare overt reference to Christianity. Yet, as will be shown, Gene's code contained morals and ethics that are completely consistent with Biblical teachings. Regarding the reinforcement of the ideals in his cowboy code in the show's episodes, Gene seemed to be an example of the cliché, "actions speak louder than words."

In the July, 1951 issue of *Radio Television Mirror* magazine, boys and girls were invited to enter a contest that involved submitting their hand-drawn artwork depicting Gene demonstrating one of the rules of his cowboy code. The description of the contest included a listing of the rules making up Gene's "Code of the West," and was preceded by the following. "Looking and living the part of a cowboy isn't enough. A fearless, honest cowboy has high ideals. No matter what the circumstances, he has the courage to stick by his code. This is my code and I'm mighty proud to pass it along to you."

1. The Cowboy must never shoot first, hit a smaller man, or take unfair advantage.

The ideals expressed in this first article of Gene's code were present in nearly all television western series – both the B Westerns and the so-called "adult" westerns. Much of the dramatic tension in a story came about because the viewer knew that when facing down the bad guy, Matt Dillon would not shoot first! This article includes the prohibition of behaviors that could lead to murder ("never shoot first"), bullying ("hit a smaller man"), or compromising one's integrity ("unfair advantage").

Gene Autry, as the cowboy hero in his series, preferred peaceful, non-violent resolutions to any sort of conflict. However, in many episodes, the attempt of some villain to take unfair advantage of a smaller or weaker individual usually draws Gene into a fight. In the episode, "The Fight at Peaceful Mesa," Gene and Pat are casually riding on the trail when they come upon a gunfight already in progress. They pull up and Pat asks Gene, "Whose side are we on?" Gene answers: "I don't know. We'll have to find out which side is right and which side is wrong." Gene and his sidekick wanted to always be sure they were fighting to defend a person who was in the right. Their intentions were consistent with the Old Testament statement in Micah 6:8 (KJV), "He hath shewed thee, O man, what is good; and what doth the Lord require of thee, but to do justly, and to love mercy, and to walk humbly with thy God?"

In a season one episode, "The Lost Chance," Gene encounters a situation in which a "tough guy" was picking on a smaller man, Pepito, and abusing Pepito's burro, named "Amigo." Gene immediately steps in to defend the innocent Pepito and his burro. Clearly, the "tough guy" in that scene was violating the command in Proverbs 3:30 (KJV): "Strive not with a man without cause, if he have done thee no harm." Gene comes to the rescue of another man in a similar situation at the beginning of the story in the episode, "Hot Lead."

As seen in every episode in the *The Gene Autry Show*, Gene was willing to fight for the right – but only when necessary, and only by fighting in a manner consistent with his cowboy code. In "The Killer Horse" episode, Gene is a bystander watching a group of children playing together as "sheriff and outlaws." After an insult is made by one of the boys, a fight breaks out between them. Gene shortly must break up the fight when some of the boys are no longer "fighting fair."

That Gene – and virtually all television western heroes – would follow the advice of this code article when attempting to apprehend law-breakers, is actually consistent with the admonition given in II Timothy 2:24-25 (KJV): "And the servant of the Lord must not strive; but be gentle unto all men, apt to teach, patient, in meekness instructing those that oppose themselves [who are in opposition]; if God peradventure will give them repentance to the acknowledging of the truth."

2.   He must never go back on his word, or a trust confided in him.

In the Bible, God is described as being the ultimate example of not going back on one's promises. In Numbers 23:19 (KJV), the writer, speaking of God and His promises, stated: "Has he said, and will he not do it? Or has he spoken, and will he not fulfill it?" This article of Gene's code reminded children that one should always honor their promises. In the episode, "The Old Prospector," Gene and Pat try to help an old prospector, who as it turns out, has been operating as a con-man for years. Gene and

Pat then try to convince the old prospector he should now go straight, as Gene tells him: "You can't go on cheatin' people forever. Sooner or later, you get caught up with." Failing to follow through on a promise leaves the other party feeling cheated, empty and abandoned, or, as described in Proverbs 25:14 (ESV): "Like clouds and wind without rain is a man who boasts of a gift he does not give."

Gene is seen by the son of the chief of a nearby tribe as a trusted friend to his father, his family, and his tribe, in the episode, "The Portrait of White Cloud." When trouble breaks out, Gene feels compelled to get involved on behalf of the tribe rather than be seen as one betraying a confidence or trust. Proverbs 20:6 (ESV) points out that "Many a man proclaims his own steadfast love, but a faithful man who can find?" This article of Gene's code points out the need to be a trustworthy individual to those with whom we interact, our families, friends, and neighbors. The writer in Proverbs 25:19 (NLT) gave a vivid picture of the one who is unreliable in time of need: "Putting confidence in an unreliable person in times of trouble is like chewing with a broken tooth or walking on a lame foot." As seen in the story, "Frame For Trouble," one may have a good name and reputation, but that is not a substitute for doing the right thing in every situation. In the Bible, Joseph was a good example of this when, having earned the confidence of his master, Potiphar, he refused to give in to a temptation that would have betrayed that trust and confidence (see Genesis 39:9).

3. He must always tell the truth.

In a season one episode, "The Doodle Bug," Pat Buttram explains to an inquisitive young boy that "doodle bug" is another name for a divining rod. The boy's next question is why it is called "divine." Pat's answer: "Because it always tells the truth – which is more'n you can say for mortal man."

Telling the truth is, of course, expected behavior of all individuals according to numerous scriptures. It is one of the Ten Commandments given in Exodus 20:16 (KJV), "You shall not bear false witness against your neighbor" – frequently quoted as, "You shall not lie." The writer in Proverbs warned, "A false witness will not go unpunished, and he who breathes out lies will not escape." (Proverbs 19:5, KJV).

Gene and his sidekicks meet up with a little girl who has a habit of telling lies in the episode, "T.N.T." In order to get her way, she makes up a lie about being kidnapped, resulting in Gene's arrest. After Sagebrush punishes her by washing her mouth out with soap, the girl admits to the sheriff that she had lied to him about being kidnapped. By the end of the story, the little girl has learned the virtue of telling the truth.

4.   He must be gentle with children, the elderly, and animals.

In the episode titled, "Hot Lead," Gene's sidekick, Tiny, watched as Gene calmed a wild horse, then remarked to Gene: "he sure was a bad horse." Gene responded, "There's no such thing as a bad horse, any more than there's a bad boy – there's just a bad way of handlin' them."

As observed in other episodes, Gene was quick to defend any child, woman, elderly person, or animal that was being mistreated. In the episode, "Johnny Jackaroo," Gene at one point states: "Horses are a lot like people – treat 'em right, and they behave. Treat 'em wrong, and they act up."

Gene's code – and behavior – echoed scriptures like I Timothy 5:1-2 (ESV), "Do not rebuke an older man but encourage him as you would a father, younger men as brothers, older women as mothers, younger women as sisters, in all purity," and Proverbs 12:10, "A righteous man regardeth the life of his beast." Honoring the aged was also commanded in Leviticus 19:32, and in the New Testament we find these instructions: "In the same way, you younger men must accept the authority of the elders. And all of you, serve each other in humility, for 'God opposes the proud but favors the humble.'" (I Peter 5:5, NLT).

Gene's specific inclusion of the elderly is unique among the various cowboy codes. Respecting the elderly was the subject of some action in the episode, "The Carnival Comes West," when Gene comes to the rescue of an older man being beat up by two thugs, one of whom claims Gene was butting into something that was none of his business. Gene retorted, "When I see someone beating on an old man, I make it my business!"

Every kid watching *The Gene Autry Show* knew Gene, who owned the beautiful and smart Champion, would not mistreat animals. In the episode, "The Killer Horse," Gene defends a wild horse that is thought to be guilty of killing a couple of men. Gene tells the men in the community they are rushing to judgment:

"Here's a horse whose life is at stake and he deserves a chance the same as you or me. A horse's life, a man's life, they're both important to this cattle country. And in a way, a horse is a man's life. He plows the ground, he works the cattle. He'll save a man's life when they're lost in the forest, or lead him to a water hole on the desert when they're both dying of thirst." (dialogue from episode, "The Killer Horse." *The Gene Autry Show*).

In another episode, "Ghost Ranch," the entire storyline has nothing to do with catching criminals – it involves Gene desperately attempting to prevent the separation of Champ from Little Champ. Gene feared a separation would cause the horse to become heart-broken in spirit.

5.   He must not advocate or possess racially or religiously intolerant ideas.

While most all of the TV cowboy codes and creeds include an article related to general respect for others, always exhibiting courtesy and good manners, and so on, Autry's specific mention of racial and religious tolerance is unique to his cowboy code.

The Bible teaches racial tolerance, since by default, all people are members of the human race, and therefore, equally created and loved by God. For example, in Genesis, we read that all living humans have the same mother (see Genesis 3:20), for ultimately, Eve "was the mother of all the living." Malachi 2:10 poses the rhetorical question, "Have we not all one father?" Then in the New Testament, we see in Acts 17:26 (ESV) that God "made from one man every nation of mankind to live on all the face of the earth, having determined allotted periods and the boundaries of their dwelling place." As seen in the teachings of Jesus, the Bible teaches going beyond racial "tolerance" by presenting the expectation of showing love toward all men. Peter, the first to take the Christian message to the non-Jews, told his colleagues: "Truly I understand that God shows no partiality, but in every nation anyone who fears Him and does what is right is acceptable to Him." (Acts 10:34-35, ESV).

In various episodes, Gene was seen to partner with people of non-white ethnicities: with Native Americans in various episodes, including "The Poisoned Waterhole," and "Blazeaway;" with a boy of African-American descent in "Six-Shooter Sweepstakes;" and Hispanics in "Guns Below the Border." In "Blazeaway," a nearby tribe of Indians is being accused of some recent killings in the area. The town's mayor does not believe their claim of innocence since he believes an Indian's word is not reliable. Gene sets him straight, telling him that a man's integrity and character is not related to outward appearances: "A man's color has nothing to do with it. It's what's inside him."

Racial tolerance is promoted again in the episode, "Ride Ranchero." In this story, Gene operates the Flying A Ranch, a ranch for troubled boys based on the principle of "the second chance." In the ranch's school, the boys get a history lesson in which they learn that Mexicans and Indians are the "original Americans," with full rights to participate along with all contemporary Americans in exercising free speech and receiving a formal classroom education.

Outside of the TV series, Gene lived out this article of his cowboy code, as well. The following message from Gene appeared in an issue of *Scholastic Magazine*, which was distributed widely throughout American schools at the time:

> Out our way a fellow has to judge a man pretty well – if he expects to stay healthy. Life in the West shows what stuff your sidekick is made of in a hurry. That's why cowboys pick their pals by what they are – not by race, religion or where they came from. Those fellows sure have no truck with prejudice of any kind – they can't afford to. (*Scholastic Magazine*, undated).

Gene Autry's signature appeared below the message.

With regard to religious tolerance, the Golden Rule again applies. The Bible also teaches God is the ultimate judge, so we should not judge, lest we be judged (Matthew 7:1), and in Romans 14:1 (ESV), Paul instructs Christians, "as for the one who is weak in faith, welcome him, but not to quarrel over opinions." Peter also wrote for Christians to "Keep your conduct among the Gentiles honorable, so that when they speak against you as evildoers, they may see your good deeds and glorify God on the day of visitation." (I Peter 2:12, ESV). The Bible also teaches Christians, "If possible, so far as it depends on you, live peaceably with all" (Romans 12:18, ESV), and to "work at living in peace with everyone, and work at living a holy life, for those who are not holy will not see the Lord." (Hebrews 12:14, NLT).

6.   He must help people in distress.

Helping those in distress of some sort was the basic motivation to action in all of the episodes of *The Gene Autry Show*. Often, Gene found himself helping children who were in trouble of some kind, as in the story of the episode, "The Star Toter," in which Gene takes in young Jimmy, a 10-year old wayward son of an outlaw. While many adults in the community thought Jimmy to be a lost cause, Gene disagreed and planned to reform the lad from the poor upbringing the father had provided.

There are times when helping others in distress may involve taking on a certain level of risk. For example, in "The Breakup," Gene was helping a suspect who was running from the law. While Gene knew that "running away from trouble doesn't solve anything," he urged the suspect – whom he knew to be innocent – to temporarily hide from the pursuing posse. "There's a difference between courage and plain stubbornness," counseled Gene.

Scriptural support for this article of Gene's cowboy code can be found in many places. For example, in I Thessalonians 5:14 (NLT): "Encourage those who are timid. Take tender care of those who are weak. Be patient with everyone." At times, helping those in distress may involve sharing resources or financial assistance, as mentioned in Acts 11:29 (ESV): "So the disciples determined, every one according to his ability, to send relief to the brothers living in Judea."

7.   He must be a good worker.

"For we hear that some among you walk in idleness, not busy at work, but busybodies. Now such persons we command and encourage in the Lord Jesus Christ to do their work quietly and to earn their own living." (II Thessalonians 3:11-12, ESV). As mentioned previously in discussing Roy Rogers' Riders Club Rules, work was a part of the human experience beginning with Adam (see Genesis 2). There are some good examples in the Old Testament of people who were good workers, even when they were not in the job they would have chosen for themselves. Joseph was such a good worker, he received promotions and higher levels of responsibility (see Genesis 39:4-6). Daniel served the king's staff in such an impeccable manner that even his most ardent detractors were unable to find legitimate grounds for dismissing him (see Daniel 6:4).

In the TV series, Gene was always portrayed as a worker, although his particular job in any given story varied among several occupations. His sidekick, Pat Buttram, likewise was always working at something – either a hired hand or attempting some business venture.

In the episode, "The Lost Chance," Pepito was hoping to locate a legendary gold mine. It turned out to be a joke, as there was no gold mine. Pepito told Gene he learned a lesson from his experiences: "Don't follow foolish ideas and try to get something for nothing."

Gene affirmed Pepito's words of wisdom, adding his own: "Now you're talking. Remember nobody ever gives you anything for nothing." Gene then tells him that he and Pat will use the reward money for catching the criminals to send Pepito to school.

8.   He must keep himself clean in thought, speech, action, and personal habits.

Several scriptures can be cited to go along with this article of Gene's cowboy code. On keeping one's self clean in: *thought* – "Finally, brothers, whatever is true, whatever is honorable, whatever is just, whatever is pure, whatever is lovely, whatever is commendable, if there is any excellence, if there is anything worthy of praise, think about these things." (Philippians 4:8, ESV); *speech* – "Let no corrupting talk come out of your mouths, but only such as is good for building up, as fits the occasion, that it may give grace to those who hear." (Ephesians 4:29, ESV); *action* – "Even a child makes himself known by his acts, by whether his conduct is pure and upright." (Proverbs 20:11, ESV); and *personal habits* – "Don't be drunk with wine, because that will ruin your life. Instead, be filled with the Holy Spirit." (Ephesians 5:18, NLT).

In "Six-Shooter Sweepstakes," Pat gets swept up in the moment and loses Champ in a bet. When he tries to explain himself to Gene, Gene asks him, "have you been drinking?"

Pat answers, "Gene, you know I don't touch that stuff!" The story addresses the folly of gambling, a theme repeated in other later episodes, as well.

In "Return of Maverick Dan," Gene tells a young girl: "No good ever came to anyone from gambling." Again, in an episode titled, "The Golden Chariot," Gene reminds Pat he does not approve of gambling.

Keeping clean as a personal habit was alluded to multiple times in various episodes, sometimes comically. In "Twisted Trails," Gene takes in a young boy, Eddie Baker, who had been hiding in a barn. Gene offers to give Eddie a meal, but insists – in spite of Eddie's protests – that Eddie needs a bath first! In the episode, "Hot Lead," before eating their meal (outdoors at their campsite) Gene is seen washing his hands and Jeff, the young boy in camp, is told he cannot eat until after he washes up.

In a first-season episode, "The Killer Horse," while Gene's sidekick, Tiny, is splashing on some cologne he had purchased in town, he tells Chuck: "This here is better than a bath."

Gene objects, saying: "You're teachin' him bad tricks. There's nothin' better than soap and water."

Tiny jokes in response: "No fun me takin' a bath . . . (he laughs) . . . can't sing!"

This kind of stuff mattered to adult viewers, judging by the letters Gene received in those days. One parent wrote asking Gene to include a hand-washing scene before sitting down to a meal, "because I'm trying to teach my children to do that and they imitate everything you do." Another letter came from a schoolteacher who always watched *The Gene Autry Show* and noticed in the sponsor spot that Gene performed, Gene would casually unwrap a stick of gum and let the paper fall to the ground. "Please roll up the wrapper and put it in your pocket, if there isn't a trash can or a wastebasket handy," she wrote. "My pupils all watch you, and I'm trying to teach them not to litter floors and streets." Gene complied with the request, once it was pointed out, according to the same 1954 article in *Radio-TV Mirror*.

9.   He must respect women, parents, and his nation's laws.

In *The Gene Autry Show* series, Gene always was respectful in his interactions with parents and the parent-child relationship, and was always fighting to uphold respect for the law. In the episode, "The Western Way," Gene pleads with the local sheriff to let him keep a young man – who inadvertently was involved in a recent bank robbery - out of jail until after Mother's Day. The mother, an elderly woman at this point, has been eagerly anticipating a visit by her son, and Gene wants her to be able to enjoy Mother's Day without the cloud of suspicion over her son's whereabouts and activities. Later, while the young man is on the run, Gene again speaks with the suspect's mother: "Ya know, ma, in this country everybody has the right to live the way they want to – as long as they respect the rights of their neighbors. That's what the law is for – to make sure they do that." This particular episode's story touched on all three components of this article in Gene's code.

In another story, "The Star Toter," Gene counseled a young boy, Jimmy, that it was important for children and parents to show mutual respect for each other by being faithful to carry out their individual responsibilities to one another. In a private conversation with the boy, Gene told him:

"Loyalty's a wonderful thing, Jimmy, and it works two ways – when you give it, you're entitled to get it in return. Now take, for instance, a kid that's loyal to his dad. His dad has to be the same way with his kid. Being loyal to his kid means teaching him to be on the square – and on the level - to make him understand the rights of other people and to respect the laws that protect all of us. See what I mean?" (dialogue from episode, "The Star Toter." *The Gene Autry Show*).

The boy admitted that if his beloved horse was stolen, he would certainly want to put the guilty man in jail. Gene pointed out that is only possible if there are laws in place to allow it. Gene, trying to convince the boy that laws are put in place for the good of everyone, pressed the point: "A man who breaks the law is going against the very things that were made to protect you, and me, and all of us."

The themes in this part of Gene's code are also commonly seen in other cowboy's codes, and are consistent with Biblical teachings. The Ten Commandments include the command to "Honor your father and your mother," (Exodus 20:12, ESV), and the instruction given to Christians in I Peter 2:17 (ESV) is to: "Honor everyone. Love the brotherhood. Fear God. Honor the emperor." Again, in Titus 3:1 (ESV), we are reminded "to be submissive to rulers and authorities."

In the New Testament, we are told to regard "governors as sent by [God] to punish those who do evil and to praise those who do good." (I Peter 2:14, ESV). In most of the TV series' episodes, Gene and Pat – acting as agents of law enforcement – are primarily engaged in upholding law and order by bringing the "bad men" to justice, while working to protect and defend those who have been wrongfully treated. As is stated in Romans 13:2 (ESV), "Therefore whoever resists the authorities resists what God has appointed, and those who resist will incur judgment." In the episode, "Killer's Trail," Gene helps a group of outlaws who were nice people who had never harmed anyone physically, but were guilty of possession of stolen property. Gene and Pat became friends with the group, but Gene convinced them it was better that they be submissive to the due process of the law and trust the justice system for leniency rather than spend a lifetime "on the dodge." At the end of the story, the group's compliance with the law – and Gene's faith in the justice system – is rewarded when the governor pardons them, setting them free.

Gene and Pat were not above the law, either, as illustrated humorously in "Cold Decked." Pat is seen enjoying his chance to do some fishing, but as the camera pans back, we see a "no fishing" sign posted in the area in which he is fishing. Just after Pat catches a fish, the game warden arrives to levy a five dollar fine. Pat admits he had seen the sign, but had chosen to ignore it. He has to pay the fine.

10. The Cowboy is a patriot.

On the front porch of a local business in town, Pat Buttram is surrounded by a group of young boys who are hanging on every word of the exciting Wild West tales he is telling, in the episode, "Dry Gulch at Devil's Elbow." Pat was telling them stories about the fantastic deeds of famous western outlaws. After a while, Gene and the sheriff walk up on the group and listen for a while, before Gene interrupts Pat with a question: "Pat, what are you holdin' out on these kids for?"

Pat asks, "What do ya mean holdin' out on 'em?"

Gene then suggests, "Why don't you tell 'em some of the stories about the real heroes of the West – true stories of the law men who were responsible for those outlaws 'dying with their boots on'!"

This episode, or at least this part of it, touches on the value of knowing about the past heroes of one's nation. It not only serves the purposes of "patriotism," but more importantly provides an identity.

Rather than citing specific verses in the Bible, we can consider the theme of patriotism as observed in the Biblical record. This idea of patriotism – at least in the sense of a people group having an identity – is seen throughout the Bible in the history of the Israelites. We see the sequence of significant events in Israel's history, such as their wars, victories, defeats, periods of captivity, economic highs and lows, and the exploits of national icons like Moses, David, and Daniel. The Israelites could also boast of national heroes like Joshua, Samson, Saul, David's "mighty men," Queen Esther, and men like Nehemiah and Ezra, who heroically led the efforts to rebuild Jerusalem's walls and its temple. Throughout their long history, even while in extended periods of captivity, the Israelites faithfully maintained their identity, in part by continuing to observe their national, annual feasts and holidays.

In a schoolroom scene in the episode, "Ride Ranchero," Gene is seen, along with the teachers and the students, beginning the school day by standing, facing the flag of the United States, and respectfully reciting the "Pledge of Allegiance." In another episode, "Six-Shooter Sweepstakes," Gene and Pat are happily participating in the festivities of the local community's July 4th celebrations. Gene also welcomes a lady who has just arrived in the West, proudly describing the West as a "land of opportunity," in the episode, "Hot Lead and Old Lace." Gene got involved in local politics in the episode, "Boots and Ballots," wherein he sought to ensure the election was conducted honorably. Gene wanted his candidate to win, but as a patriot, it was important to win without using unethical tactics. He said, "If you can't win fair and square, it's no good."

Throughout the TV series, Gene exemplified the role of "patriot" in a manner summed up succinctly in I Peter 2:17 (ESV): "Honor everyone. Love the brotherhood. Fear God. Honor the emperor."

A Role Model

Unlike some other cowboy codes and creeds, Gene Autry's Cowboy Code of Honor did not specifically include a mention of either education, or of God or church, in any of its articles. However, both themes are present in various episodes of the TV series.

In the episode, "Galloping Hoofs," the local school is in need of new desks for the students and Gene is involved with the fund raising efforts. Gene tells the sheriff this work is important because, "There's nothing more important than education, sheriff."

Pat Buttram is less enthusiastic, since, he says, "I never went to school, and it don't bother me none."

Gene's response: "Well, book-learning may seem a waste of time, Pat, but the fellow who won't take advantage of all the education he can get is just plain foolish."

The "opportunity cost" of a lack of education was illustrated in the episode, "Ghost Mountain." In this story, an outlaw group has chosen a hideout location that also happens to be the site of a valuable, historic treasure. However, due to their lack of knowledge about the history of the area, they are not aware of this fact. After the outlaws have been captured at their hideout, Professor Donald Markham says, "Well, if they'd only known it – they had a fortune right here in their hands."

Gene then summarizes: "Which just proves that it pays to know your history. In it, you find some of the greatest stories in the world. Every page you read, you meet men like Coronado and Columbus."

In Gene's Cowboy Code, there is no direct reference to God or church, yet in a few episodes we see that a spiritual component did exist in Gene's character. In the episode, "Talking Guns," Gene and a young boy named Ronnie are captured by outlaws and tied up in chairs. A worried Ronnie asks, "What are we going to do, Mr. Autry?"

Gene suggests: "When you're tied up, it's not a bad idea to start prayin'. You don't know how much power there is in prayer until you've tried it, Ronnie."

Ronnie says, "The only prayin' I know is, 'now I lay me down to sleep.'"

Gene assures him: "You don't have to know any prayers. All you have to do is talk in your heart – like talking into a telephone. It'll be answered."

Ronnie then proceeds to humbly offer a prayer asking for help for himself and Gene.

The usefulness of prayer was also mentioned in "Thunder Out West," after Gene and Pat successfully execute a plan to trap the outlaws. The preacher tells Gene that during the time Gene and Pat were putting their plan into action, he and two of the robbery victims had been at the church praying for the success of the plan.

In a story that may have been one of the best mystery stories told in Gene's TV series, the Ten Commandments are an important key to the plot. The episode is "Ransom Cross." In the story, a cross is stolen, and the thieves demand a ransom for its return. It is at the end of the story, when the stolen cross – the treasured artifact the two archeologists had worked so hard to find – had been recovered, that Gene and Pat learn it was one of a set of ten, each representing one of the Ten Commandments. The inscription on this one was "Thou shalt not steal," written in Spanish.

As mentioned earlier, Gene managed to sing at least one song in every episode of his TV series. In some instances, the song he performs has lyrics based in Biblical values. For example, in "Revenge Trail," Gene performs "Silver Spurs (On The Golden Stairs)," which has lines like, *You've got to ride the right road brother/ Make your sins all skedaddle/ Get old Satan out of your saddle/ If you wanna clink your silver spurs upon the golden stairs.* In the episode, "Law Comes to Scorpion," Gene is seen in church singing along with the congregation the hymn, "Somebody Bigger Than You and I." The lyrics are:

Who made the mountains, who made the trees / Who made the rivers flow to the sea / And who sends the rain when the earth is dry / Somebody bigger than you and I / Who made the flowers to bloom in the spring / Who made the song for the robins to sing / And who hung the moon and the stars in the sky / Somebody bigger than you and I / He lights the way when the road is long / He keeps you company / And with his love to guide you / He walks beside you / Just like he walks with me / When we're filled with despair / Who gives me courage to go from there / And who gives me faith that will never die / Somebody bigger than you and I.

Gene Autry accepted the fact that he was a role model and that his public persona mattered in the minds of his fans, especially the younger fans. He apparently took this responsibility seriously, as evidenced by his own words:

If your youngster has a faith to live by he'll never wander off the trail. As any cowhand will tell you, it's easier to keep 'em on a well-marked trail than to hunt for a maverick once he's wandered away. Even when you find 'em, they don't always want to come back. It's like that with youngsters. Give them a trail to follow – something to guide them when problems come along – and you'll never have a maverick on your hands. Even when the grazing looks greener away from the path, if your kids are sure the path leads to something – even though they can't see the destination – they'll stick to it. It's all in believing – having faith. I guess that's the biggest gift any parent can give a child – and it's more valuable than anything money can buy. (Rothel, *The Gene Autry Book*).

Photo from inside front cover of *Gene Autry Comics*, Dell Comics, October, 1950.

The ten points of Gene Autry's "Code of the West" was at the heart of the contest promoted in "Gene Autry Prize Round-Up," *Radio Television Mirror*, July, 1951. Gene told the readers: "Looking and living the part of a cowboy isn't enough. A fearless, honest cowboy has high ideals. No matter what the circumstances, he has the courage to stick by his code. This is my code and I'm mighty proud to pass it along to you."

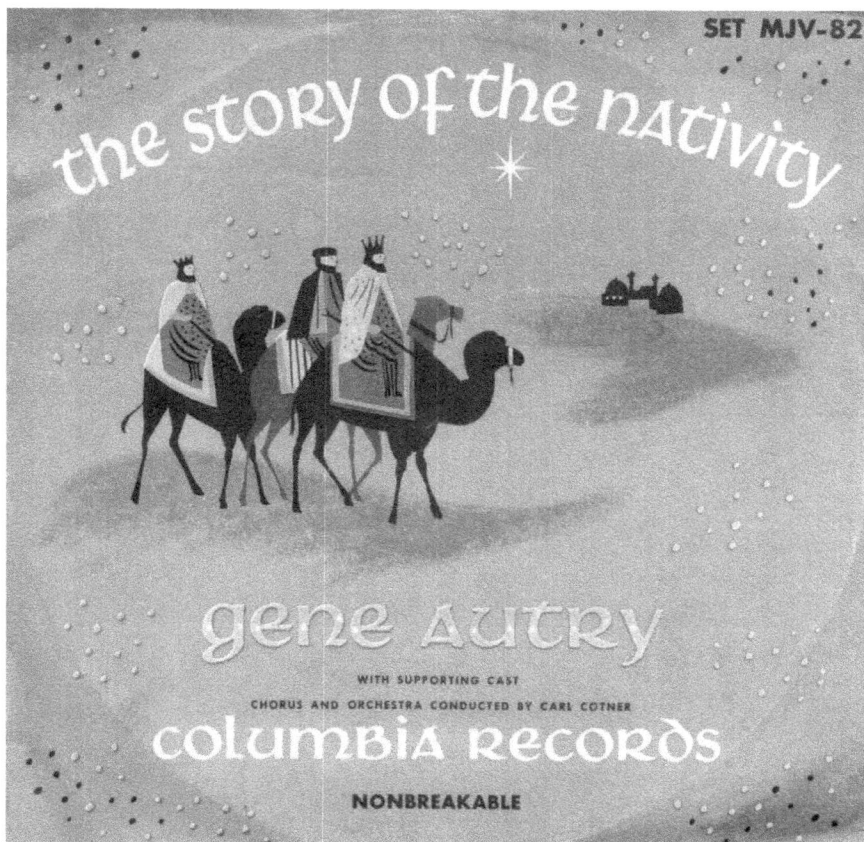

Album cover from one of many Christmas-themed albums released by Gene Autry.

4

HOPALONG CASSIDY

OPENING CREDITS

"Here he comes, here he comes / There's the trumpets, there's the drums, here he comes / Hopalong Cassidy, here he comes," sang a chorus of voices as Hopalong Cassidy rode into view on the small screen in millions of homes each week.

The Good Guy in the Black Hat

Younger readers may have little or no awareness of the early television phenomenon that was Hopalong Cassidy, the first western hero to regularly appear on television. In November, 1948, Hopalong Cassidy films began to appear on a regular weekly basis in the New York market, and attracted enough viewers that NBC quickly made a deal with William "Hopalong Cassidy" Boyd to feature his films as part of the network's prime time programming. The cowboy craze termed by some as "Hoppymania" was the immediate result, and, with his nationally syndicated radio show and TV programs airing weekly, Boyd was for a couple of years, as described by author John Dunning, "as big a media hero as the nation had seen."

By February, 1950, sales of Hopalong Cassidy comic books were reported to be around 14 million comics, and by July, 1950, total tie-in merchandise sales totals were expected to reach the $20 million mark for 1950 (*Sponsor*, July, 1950). The November 27, 1950, *TIME* magazine issue, reported on the extent to which Hopalong had saturated the market: "Last week 63 television stations were pumping out his old movies, 152 radio stations were carrying his voice, 155 newspapers were printing his new Hopalong Cassidy comic strip, and 108 licensed manufacturers were turning out Hopalong Cassidy products at the rate of $70 million a year."

Hopalong Cassidy was featured on the cover of the June 12, 1950, issue of *LIFE* magazine. The article inside aptly described the celebrity status the character had achieved:

> ...the cowboy juggernaut penetrates every dwelling which has young children – through television, radio or mere juvenile conversation; in records, comic strips, Hoppy books and Hoppy clubs; via cowboy clothes, breakfast food, blankets, towels, bedcovers, lamps, watches, bicycles, candy, soap and even wallpaper – and American youth is more aware of Hoppy than earlier generations ever were of Buffalo Bill, Lindbergh, Babe Ruth or other idols of the past. The objection that Hopalong is a fictional character is swept away at once; Hoppy is visible flesh and blood, who has merged with and absorbed completely the formerly separate personality of William Lawrence Boyd, actor. (*LIFE*, June 12, 1950).

The article also noted that in personal appearances throughout the country, Hopalong was always met by tens of thousands of excited fans. Huge crowds waited to see him in personal appearances at department stores in Brooklyn and Philadelphia, at a parade in New Orleans, and at the Cole Brothers' Circus in Chicago. There were other popular characters from children's programs in early television, such as Howdy Doody and Captain Video, but no one was a bigger television star than Hopalong Cassidy.

Being first in an endeavor has its advantages, and that was certainly the case for William "Hopalong Cassidy" Boyd. Having risked all of his personal wealth to invest in the Hopalong Cassidy films and the character property rights, Boyd gambled on the new medium of television – and won. No one yet knew of the commercial viability of television programming, but Boyd made his Hopalong films available for broadcast and the early TV stations – eager for material to fill the available hours of airtime – played his films repeatedly. The March, 1949, issue of *Radio and Television Mirror* contained this note on television programming: "And if you're a 'Hopalong

Cassidy' fan, you have probably been having a wonderful time these early winter Sunday evenings watching that rootin' tootin' character played by Bill Boyd."

Boyd did not manage to get made-for-TV episodes of Hopalong on television until 1952, but by previously getting edited versions of his movies on the air ahead of the other western heroes, he was able to capture the hearts of millions of young television viewers. "Why a man of 52 years appealed to so many children remains a mystery," wrote Dunning. "Possibly some of it had to do with the novelty of television . . . a TV sensation was bound to occur."

The Hopalong Cassidy character originated in the writings of novelist Clarence E. Mulford. In Mulford's stories, Hopalong was more similar to the historical version of the American cowboy. He dressed in ragged clothing, chewed tobacco, and used earthy language. Mulford's character also walked with a bad limp – hence the name "Hopalong."

William Boyd first played the character of Hopalong Cassidy in sixty-six films, beginning in the 1930s. However, Boyd began to adapt the character into a different mold, becoming more personally identified with the character in the process. Boyd succeeded in turning Hopalong into "a soft-spoken paragon who did not smoke, drink, or kiss girls, who tried to capture the rustlers instead of shooting them, and who always let the villain draw first if gunplay was inevitable."(*TIME*, November 27, 1950). Boyd told one interviewer, "I knew Hoppy was something I could do good with." (*TV-Radio Mirror*, February, 1950). With an eye toward the coming of

"When Boyd went on a personal-appearance tour across the U.S., he was constantly surrounded by fearsome crowds; 85,000 people rushed through a Brooklyn department store in four short hours simply to take a look at him, and 350,000 people jammed mid-Manhattan streets when he appeared outside the New York Daily News building to advertise the Hopalong Cassidy comic strip."

(*TIME*, November 27, 1950)

television, and his passion for the character, Boyd began to use all of his accumulated savings and assets to purchase the complete rights to the Hopalong character and obtain ownership of all the Hopalong films.

By this approach, taking great personal financial risk, Boyd was able to be the first cowboy hero on television, with edited-for-TV versions of his movies airing on NBC-TV on Sunday nights, with Silver Cup Bread for General Foods as his sponsor. He had no competition on television initially, until *The Cisco Kid* and *The Lone Ranger* began broadcasting their made-for-TV films.

The use of edited Hopalong films was a huge success, as described earlier, but as more western competition arrived, Boyd began producing his own made-for-TV Hopalong Cassidy films which began airing in 1952. These half-hour made-for-TV episodes make up what is now considered the *Hopalong Cassidy* series. The show managed to maintain the high level of popularity of the Hopalong character and associated merchandising. One western writer described the show in hindsight in this manner:

> There is universal agreement among television historians that the quality of the made-for-television *Hopalong Cassidy* programs left much to be desired. Scripts were weakly written. Action sequences minimal or non-existent. The shooting of outdoor scenes outdoors instead of in studio sound stages lent an air of quality to otherwise drab and dreary looking locations. None of this mattered. Millions of youngsters watched and adored Hoppy. (Rinker, *Hopalong Cassidy – King of the Cowboy Merchandisers*).

The *Hopalong Cassidy* made-for-TV series began airing on television in 1952, and continued for 52 episodes over two broadcast seasons before going into reruns. Hopalong owned the Bar-20 ranch and typically served as a marshal at Twin Rivers who was frequently called upon by some level of locally operating law enforcement officials or to assist the army in uncovering criminal behavior. At other times, he is seen coming to the aid of the elderly, widows, or someone else in a desperate situation. Quite often the stories are presented in such a manner that the viewer does not know the identity of the main criminal until the end, making it something of a true cowboy detective show. Like the other B Western heroes, Hopalong is accompanied in his adventures by a trusted sidekick who also provides a measure of comic relief in the show. Hopalong had two sidekicks in the first dozen episodes – California and Lucky. However, his main sidekick in the show was the grumpy Red Connors, played by veteran actor Edgar Buchanan, now more remembered for his later role as Uncle Joe in *Petticoat Junction*.

Hoppy, as portrayed by William Boyd, was an older man with white hair, wearing a black outfit with a black hat, who rode a white horse, and had an easily recognized laugh to go with a distinct voice that conveyed a sense of authority and power. The extensive narration by Hoppy in each episode added to that sense of authority and power – the feeling of a "wise uncle" who was in charge of the situation. Boyd intentionally played Hoppy as a likeable mentoring-type character who respected the intelligence of his audience: "I don't treat the kids as kids – they don't like that – I play to the adults. That pleases everybody" (*LIFE*, June 12, 1950). Interestingly, an estimated 46% of the *Hopalong Cassidy* audience was adults.

In resolving the conflict in any given story, Hoppy's decisions and actions, like the other B-Western heroes, followed a high moral code of conduct. Additional insight into how this moral compass guided his actions was provided with the extensive use of voice-over narration in the episodes. With this device, Hopalong had the unique opportunity to frequently make observations or comments on his and Red's thought processes about people and events. The use of narration during ordinary riding scenes – rather than lots of action sequences – may actually have served to give the show a more intellectual aura, relative to the other B-Western shows. As one western film writer noted, "Hoppy used brains, not brawn to solve the puzzles that he and his companions faced." (Rinker, *Hopalong Cassidy – King of the Cowboy Merchandisers*).

With the incredible success of his television shows, Boyd was keenly aware of the impact he was having on American youth, and he felt a great personal responsibility to his audience. "Boyd—who, at 55, is an erect, ruddy man with a direct gaze, a quick smile, and a surprising air of authority and command—now has an almost evangelistic attitude about his success. He . . . seems to feel that he has re-tapped the same deep vein of American character which made the Old West, and that it is both his fate and his duty to strengthen the fiber of U.S. youth" (*TIME*, November 27, 1950). In real life, Boyd was careful to maintain a public persona consistent with the Hopalong Cassidy image. "Bill never drinks or smokes because, he says, 'I'll never willingly disillusion one person who believes in Hoppy'" (*TV-Radio*

Mirror, February, 1950).

It is difficult here to fully convey the extent to which Hoppy influenced the American culture in the early 1950s. However, Cecil B. DeMille was not overstating things when he was interviewed about Hopalong Cassidy for a December, 1950, article in *Coronet* magazine: "Every kid needs a hero. Hopalong Cassidy takes the place of Buffalo Bill, Babe Ruth, Lindy and all the rest. He's everything that young America admires and wants." An article in *The American Weekly* noted: "Today more children are influenced by Hoppy's code than any other single factor in America." (The two previous quotes taken from Rinker's *Hopalong Cassidy: King of the Cowboy Merchandisers*.) "Hoppymania" was observable throughout the country, and Boyd took advantage of the opportunity to be a role model – the heroic knight on the white horse.

Creed for American Boys and Girls

1. The highest badge of honor a person can wear is honesty. Be truthful at all times.
2. Your parents are the best friends you have. Listen to them and obey their instructions.
3. If you want to be respected, you must respect others. Show good manners in every way.
4. Only through hard work and study can you succeed. Don't be lazy.
5. Your good deeds always come to light. So don't boast or be a show-off.
6. If you waste time or money today, you will regret it tomorrow. Practice thrift in all ways.
7. Many animals are good and loyal companions. Be friendly and kind to them.
8. A strong, healthy body is a precious gift. Be neat and clean.
9. Our country's laws are made for your protection. Observe them carefully.
10. Children in many foreign lands are less fortunate than you. Be glad and proud you are an American.

Like the other B Western heroes, Hopalong Cassidy embodied a hero whose character was faithful to the tenets of his Creed for American Boys and Girls in every episode of his TV series. Like Autry, "actions speak louder than words," so only minimal amounts of dialogue within the episodes directly spoke to the values expressed in Hoppy's creed. However, unique to Hopalong Cassidy's show, was the addition of episode trailers used during the second season of the series. In these trailers, Hoppy would be shown in close-up while sitting or standing in various scenes, and during which he would look directly into the camera to address his audience. He typically used this opportunity to remind children – and sometimes parents – of some point about manners, ethics, or morals that could also be found in his Creed.

1. The highest badge of honor a person can wear is honesty. Be truthful at all times.

The first article of Hopalong Cassidy's Creed for American Boys and Girls addressed honesty and truth-telling. The Bible has much to say about the virtue of honesty, and also hints at the "highest badge of honor" status upon which Hoppy confers this virtue. Proverbs 12:22 (ESV) indicates that "lying lips are an abomination" to the Lord, in contrast to those who "act faithfully" – they are the Lord's "delight." Most of the six things listed in Proverbs 6:16-20 as things that the Lord hates are directly related to lying or showing dishonor toward others. The passage states: "There are six things that the Lord hates, seven that are an abomination to him: haughty eyes, a lying tongue, and hands that shed innocent blood, a heart that devises wicked plans, feet that make haste to run to evil, a false witness who breathes out lies, and one who sows discord among brothers." (Proverbs 6:16-20, ESV). In the New Testament, Christians are instructed not to lie to one another (Colossians 3:9), and to "keep his tongue from evil and his lips from speaking deceit" (I Peter 3:10-12, ESV). The writer of Hebrews also expressed the Christian's desire "to act honorably in all things" (Hebrews 13:18, ESV).

In the episode trailer used with "New Mexico Manhunt" and "Steel Trails West," Hoppy began his message with this admonition for the younger members of his audience: "Hi, little partners! Any time you play a game, play it to win. . . ." Hoppy was reminding them that it was always important to give an honest effort in everything one attempts - even when playing games with friends and playmates.

2. Your parents are the best friends you have. Listen to them and obey their instructions.

In a trailer used with two episodes, "The Sole Survivor," and "3-7-77," Hopalong left his youthful audience with these words: "Now here's a little message for my little friends…always mind your Daddy and your Mommy. Please remember they're the best friends you have in the world. Until next week, take good care of yourselves."

This article of Hoppy's creed calls to mind a verse from the Bible that many children learned in Sunday School: "Children, obey your parents in the Lord, for this is right" (Ephesians 6:1, ESV). That Bible passage continues with a reference to one of the Ten Commandments, "'Honor your father and mother'—which is the first command with a promise—'so that it may go well with you and that you may enjoy long life on earth.'" While growing up with Joseph and Mary, Jesus himself modeled this behavior. The scriptures record that Jesus obeyed his earthly parents, and throughout his childhood grew in wisdom and favor with both God and people.

In two more episode trailers, Hoppy spoke to the children specifically about the importance of obeying their parents. At the end of "The Emerald Saint," and "The Devil's Idol," Hoppy closed with:

Hi there, little partners. I think you know your mommy is the nicest and the most beautiful woman in the world - and that she loves you very dearly. So when she asks you to do anything, don't fuss about it - just do it. For instance, when she asks you to have a glass of milk, drink it - and then surprise her by asking for another one. You try that, and see how much better you both feel. Now until next week, so long - and in the meantime, watch yourself at the crosswalks, will you? (Trailer #9, *Hopalong Cassidy* television series).

In another trailer, used with episodes "Silent Testimony" and "Death by Proxy," Hoppy reminded the kids it was important to obey their parents' instructions in a prompt manner. In this trailer, he told them:

Hi, there, little partners. I understand there's been quite a little talk around your house lately about 'going to bed.' Now I know that we all hate to go to bed. We're always so afraid we're going to miss something. But you must get a lot of sleep! And the time to go to bed is when your Mommy or your Daddy tell you to - not fifteen minutes later, or twenty minutes later, or not one or two television shows later, but right now. I'll see you next week. Until then, get lots of good sleep, will you? Good night. (Trailer #11, *Hopalong Cassidy* television series).

With this kind of messaging from Hoppy, it is easy to understand why parents were okay with allowing their children to watch *Hopalong Cassidy*!

3. If you want to be respected, you must respect others. Show good manners in every way.

In the episode, "Twisted Trails," after a woman rejoiced that the local cattlemen came to the aid of her father in his time of need, Red Connors observed: "Your dad sure had a lot of trust in them cattlemen."

Hopalong agreed with him, adding, "Red, if more men had the faith in people that he had, this world would be a much nicer place to live in."

This article of Hoppy's creed is more or less a version of the Golden Rule – "Do to others as you would like them to do to you." (Luke 6:31, NLT). The Bible also teaches the importance of this rule in the behavior and reputation of young children in Proverbs 20:11 (ESV), which states "even a child makes himself known by his acts, by whether his conduct is pure and upright."

The themes of showing good manners and being respectful of others were hit upon in multiple trailer episodes. Hoppy closed out two episodes ("New Mexico Manhunt" and "Steel Trails West") by directing children to maintain good manners toward each other during play: "Hi, little partners! Any time you play a game, play it to win. But remember, somebody always has to lose. And in case it's you, don't be unhappy about it – be a good loser. Just try a little harder the next time. I'll see you next week." (Trailer #8, *Hopalong Cassidy* television series).

Knowing that millions of children were playing with Hopalong Cassidy cap guns and other similar merchandise, Hoppy urged them to also show respect for those around them – as a matter of courtesy and safety! In the episode trailer used with "Frameup for Murder" and "The Jinx Wagon," Hoppy related this incident, followed by a warning:

Hi, there, little friends. This is just a thought about guns. I was doing a scene one time in one of the pictures and the boy that was working with me was twirling his gun on his hand and playing with it. I said, 'What are you doing with that gun, Lucky?' He said, 'I was just playing with it!' I said, 'Those things are not to play with...they kill people!' So watch your guns, children. Be careful with them, won't you? (Trailer #6, *Hopalong Cassidy* television series).

In two separate episode trailers, Hoppy extended the showing of respect to include the children's relationship with their local police officers. In one trailer, seen at the end of the episode "Double Trouble," he spoke to children and parents alike:

Hi, my little partners. There's a group of men in America that walk the streets and stand on the corners dressed in pretty good-looking uniforms. Those men look pretty smart - and I want to assure you that they are smart, or they wouldn't be there. I'm speaking of policemen! The policeman is a father – the same as some of you grown-ups are. He has children – the same as you have. And his job is to help you protect your children, and to help protect the children themselves. So keep one thing in mind, won't you, please? Don't call them a 'cop'! He's a respected man, and we should call him by a respected name - a 'police officer.' Always remember that, and see how much nicer he'll be. I'll see you next week. (Trailer #10, *Hopalong Cassidy* television series).

In the episode trailer for "The Renegade Press" and "The Outlaw's Reward," Hoppy stressed the benefits of respecting law officers:

Hi, my little partners! I want to ask you a very serious question: are you afraid of policemen? You're not, huh? Well, that's good. You shouldn't be! Always remember that those men have had a lot of training, have put in a lot of years to learn how to help protect you. And one more thing – don't ever call a policeman a 'cop'! He doesn't like it and it doesn't sound good. Respect him as he does you. Call him a 'police officer' and see how much nicer he'll be. I'll see you next week. In the meantime, don't forget to go to Sunday School. (Trailer #12, *Hopalong Cassidy* television series).

4. Only through hard work and study can you succeed. Don't be lazy.

The Bible has much to say about the need for and the rewards of honest labor, and warns of the negative consequences for laziness. In the New Testament, some rather strong language is used to state the expectation that Christians were to work to support themselves and their families: "But if anyone does not provide for his relatives, and especially for members of his household, he has denied the faith and is worse than an unbeliever." In the Old Testament book of Proverbs, the necessity of hard work and constant attentiveness to one's business ventures is seen in a passage in chapter 24, verses 30-34 (ESV): "I passed by the field of a sluggard, by the vineyard of a man lacking sense, and behold, it was all overgrown with thorns; the ground was covered with nettles, and its stone wall was broken down. Then I saw and considered it; I looked and received instruction. A little sleep, a little slumber, a little folding of the hands to rest, and poverty will come upon you like a robber, and want like an armed man." Even in the beginning, in Genesis, we see that in the midst of Paradise, the Garden of Eden, Adam had work duties to perform. Work – hard work – is simply a part of succeeding in life.

Hoppy's creed commanded that children not be lazy, echoing scriptures like Proverbs 13:4 – "The soul of the sluggard craves and gets nothing" (ESV) – and Proverbs 10:4 – "a slack hand causes poverty" (ESV). In the New Testament, we find the command, "if anyone is not willing to work, let him not eat" (II Thessalonians 3:10, ESV). Parents must have certainly appreciated the inclusion of this article in Hopalong's creed. Hoppy also addressed this directly with his young viewers in the episode trailer used with the episodes, "Tricky Fingers" and "The Last Laugh." In this trailer, Hoppy challenged the children to look for ways to be helpful around the house: "HI, little partners. Have you been doing anything to help Mom around the house lately? You haven't? Let's do all we can to help her, eh? I bet you'll have fun doing it, and I know Mom will appreciate it. Will you do that for me? Now, 'til next week, so long - and good luck!" (Trailer #1, *Hopalong Cassidy* television series).

Like other cowboy codes, Hopalong's creed included a reference to education - citing study (along with hard work) as a prerequisite for success. This advice is also noted in Proverbs 19:20 (ESV): "Listen to advice and accept instruction, that you may gain wisdom in the future." In the episode, "Borrowed Trouble," the teacher in the one-room schoolhouse was unavailable to teach one day, so Hoppy filled in as a substitute. Upon entering the schoolhouse, he immediately directed the students to their studies: "Well children, your teacher won't be here today, but this school has to keep running for a lot of reasons. I had a little concentrating to do myself, and I couldn't think of a better place to do it than in a school room. Now, uh, suppose I assign ya some lessons and we'll all settle down to some nice, quiet work."

5. Your good deeds always come to light. So don't boast or be a show-off.

In a season one episode of *Hopalong Cassidy*, "Alien Range," Hopalong helps to protect an immigrant settler and his family who have recently set up a family ranch and are in need of help. The bad guy, Simon Cosgrove, tries to scare off Hoppy: "You're asking for trouble Cassidy – sticking your nose in where it don't concern you. You're gonna get it!"

Hoppy makes it clear he will not be intimidated, telling Cosgrove: "I'll be around. Get out of here!"

At end of the story, the family expresses their heartfelt thanks to Hoppy and Red for their help. Mr. Vandemeer (the immigrant rancher) tells them, "We thank both of you for helping us in our trouble."

Both Hoppy and Red deflected the praise, as Red responded, "Oh, we had fun!"

Hoppy added, "Red and I always enjoy a fight when it's for a good cause!" Like his fellow Western heroes, Hopalong Cassidy performed good deeds because someone needed help – it was a matter of doing the right thing.

This specific creed article is unique to Hoppy, but all of the B Western TV heroes operated in this manner. In the Old Testament, we read, "Let another praise you, and not your own mouth; A stranger, and not your own lips." (Proverbs 27:2, ESV). In the New Testament, Jesus taught his disciples not to be in the business of seeking adoration from others for their good deeds, telling them in Matthew 6:2 (NLT), "When you give to someone in need, don't do as the hypocrites do—blowing trumpets in the synagogues and streets to call attention to their acts of charity! I tell you the truth, they have received all the reward they will ever get." The writer of Hebrews pointed out that one's good works are noticed by God: "For God is not unjust so as to overlook your work and the love that you have shown for his name in serving the saints, as you still do." (Hebrews 6:10, ESV).

What is special about this creed article is that it speaks to one's motives and purposes in doing good deeds. From a Biblical perspective, one should be aware that ultimately their strength, courage, and ability to "do good" comes not from themselves, but from God. In the episode, "Don't Believe in Ghosts," Hoppy helped a young boy find courage in the midst of a trial. In the story, Hoppy is trying to locate the boy's missing father, rancher Tom Murdock. The young boy, Tom's son, Billy, is hoping that Hoppy will succeed and is struggling in the meantime to remain brave. In the quiet of a late evening, Billy asks Hoppy, "Where does courage come from, Hoppy?"

Hoppy answered him thoughtfully: "Oh, Billy, I guess nobody really knows. People perform heroic deeds and they wonder where the courage came from. I think the best answer's in the Bible. It says 'be of good courage and He shall strengthen your heart all ye that hope in the Lord.'" Hoppy was quoting from Psalms 31:24.

Billy promised, "I'll remember that." The young boy apparently took that scripture to heart. In the last scene, after the banker has been arrested for the murder of the boy's father and everything resolved, Billy bids farewell to Hoppy with the whispered words: "be of good courage and He shall strengthen your heart all ye that hope in the Lord!"

6. If you waste time or money today, you will regret it tomorrow. Practice thrift in all ways.

This is another creed article with a theme that is a bit unique to Hopalong in its emphasis on thrift with regards to time and money. However, the general theme here of using one's resources wisely – with an eye to the future – was also expressed in some form in other cowboy codes, as well. In the episode trailer used with episodes "The Black Sombrero" and "Arizona Troubleshooters," Hoppy included a reminder to the kids to take responsible care of their belongings when he told them not leave behind their raincoats and overshoes at the schoolhouse.

Perhaps the best example seen in the Bible of one who used thrift specifically in planning for the future is the story of Joseph in the book of Genesis. Joseph devised and supervised the implementation of a plan to store food in advance of an anticipated period of famine in the land of Egypt. In Proverbs 6:6-8, we see the wisdom of taking personal initiative to use our time and money wisely in order to prepare for future needs: "Take a lesson from the ants, you lazybones. Learn from their ways and become wise! Though they have no prince or governor or ruler to make them work, they labor hard all summer, gathering food for the winter." (Proverbs 6:6-8, NLT).

By the early 1950s, Americans were being informed in various ways on the need for conservation and the wise use of our nation's natural resources. This theme was alluded to in a humorous manner in the episode, "Borrowed Trouble," in a conversation with a young student. Hoppy asked a little boy, "What do you want to be when you grow up?"

The little boy responded, "A Indian!"

Hopalong then asked: "An Indian. Why?"

The little boy began, "My pop says the country's in bad shape, so we could give it back to the Indians…"

Hopalong laughed aloud, interrupting him with a shake of his head: "I don't know. If we keep on with what we're doing to it, the Indians won't want it back!"

7. Many animals are good and loyal companions. Be friendly and kind to them.

As we have already noted in review of the Roy Rogers Riders Club rules and Gene Autry's code, the Bible contains verses about taking proper care of animals. For example, Proverbs 12:10 (NASB) states "A righteous man has regard for the life of his animal," and in Proverbs 27:23 (ESV), "Know well the condition of your flocks, and give attention to your herds."

In the TV series, every child knew – and witnessed for themselves – the care given by Hopalong to his famous white horse, Topper. Furthermore, whenever Hopalong (William Boyd) made personal appearances with Topper, the extravagant trailer in which Topper was transported was well known to the public at the time. Children knew that Topper was well protected and cared for.

8. A strong, healthy body is a precious gift. Be neat and clean.

Speaking directly into the camera to address the younger members of his audience in an episode trailer closing out the episode, "Gypsy Destiny," Hoppy reinforced his creed article that dealt with the theme of maintaining a healthy body:

Hi there, friends! You know sometimes a smile will buy things that money can't buy. But there's something pretty important that goes with that smile…good teeth! A lot of people worry about going to the dentist. Remember that he's just as nice a guy as any other guy and he wants to help you. So go and see him at least once a year – maybe twice a year. Brush your teeth good twice every day, too. Will you do that for me? (Trailer #13, *Hopalong Cassidy* television series).

Each of the "big three" – Roy, Gene, and Hoppy – included an article in their creeds which reminded kids of the importance of personal safety and hygiene, and being neat and clean. "Cleanliness is next to godliness" has been frequently quoted as though it is a passage from the Bible. It is not. However, the teachings found in the Bible include information on personal hygiene and even public sanitation methods. Many examples exist in scripture of people bathing or, in the case of the New Testament, caring for guests by providing for washing of the feet. As we have already seen with Roy and Gene, the Bible contains several passages dealing with these ideas. One such passage is in Leviticus 13-14, where we see that the Mosaic Law included a set of laws outlining the sanitation practices the Israelites were to follow. These laws included instructions for how to set up their camp in a clean, safe manner that could be rather specific and explicit. Consider, for example, the detail included in this Old Testament passage:

You shall have a place outside the camp, and you shall go out to it. And you shall have a trowel with your tools, and when you sit down outside, you shall dig a hole with it and turn back and cover up your excrement. Because the Lord your God walks in the midst of your camp, to deliver you and to give up your enemies before you, therefore your camp must be holy, so that he may not see anything indecent among you and turn away from you. (Deuteronomy 23:12-14, ESV).

At the end of two episodes, Hoppy spoke to the kids about the importance of using soap and water, reminding them it is an important part of staying healthy. In the episode trailer used with episodes "Twisted Trails" and "Don't Believe in Ghosts," Hopalong looked at the camera as though he could actually see the children he was addressing as he spoke:

Hi, there, my little friends. Have you been washing your face and hands good lately? How about your ears? [Hoppy pauses and looks toward one side of the camera like he is checking the viewer's ears.] They look pretty good! Don't forget that soap and water not only keeps you nice and clean, but it also protects your health. So use lots of it, won't you? I'll see you next week. (Trailer #4, *Hopalong Cassidy* television series).

Apparently, the parents in the viewing audience appreciated Hopalong's messages to their children and wrote letters to him that included suggestions for other behaviors Hoppy could address. That appears to be the origin of Hoppy's message in the episode trailer used to close the episodes, "The Black Sombrero" and "Arizona Troubleshooters." Children then and now are known to leave behind coats, hats, and gloves in their haste to move from one activity to another, so at the apparent urging of parents, Hoppy spoke to the kids:

Hi, my young friends! You know, I've had a lot of letters over the last six or eight months about you not wearing your raincoats and your overshoes. Now the reason you don't see 'Hoppy' in a raincoat and overshoes is that I live in a country where there isn't too much rain. But you must always — when it is raining — wear your raincoats and your overshoes! And there's one more thought, too…don't leave them at the schoolhouse! Bring them home, will you? I'll see you next week, and be sure and wear those, will you? (Trailer #7, *Hopalong Cassidy* television series).

Also embodied in this creed article would be the matter of personal safety. Hoppy reminded boys and girls to be aware of their surroundings while outdoors in the episode trailer used with "Copper Hills" and "Grubstake":

Hi, there, my little friends. If you were playing baseball and the baseball was knocked across a railroad track, I'm pretty sure when you got to that railroad track you'd stop, look, and listen, wouldn't you? Now please remember that any street in America is just as dangerous as that railroad - so when you get to the curbstone, stop, look, and listen. Will you do that for me? Now so long until next week - and in the meantime, don't forget to go to Sunday School. (Trailer #14, *Hopalong Cassidy* television series).

9. Our country's laws are made for your protection. Observe them carefully.

Hi, there. You know there are certain laws that are made to protect all of us…but we must do something to help about that protection. So here's a thought that might help prevent an accident. Help other people protect you. Now to make it a little easier for you to remember those words, the first letter of each of those words spell the name of a man who thinks you're pretty wonderful and who doesn't want you to be hurt. So 'til next week, so long! In the meantime, be careful, won't you? (Trailer #3, *Hopalong Cassidy* television series).

With these words in the episode trailer used to close out episodes "Masquerade for Matilda" and "Illegal Entry," Hoppy made the dual points that laws are made to protect us, but that they work only to the extent that we all obey the law.

Obeying the nation's laws is a common mantra of the cowboy creeds, and the Bible teaches that God has sanctioned human governments as a means of providing protection and justice under the law. Portions of this passage in Romans have been referenced previously, but the entire passage is instructive. It explains God's purposes for human government:

Let every person be subject to the governing authorities. For there is no authority except from God, and those that exist have been instituted by God. Therefore whoever resists the authorities resists what God has appointed, and those who resist will incur judgment. For rulers are not a terror to good conduct, but to bad. Would you have no fear of the one who is in authority? Then do what is good, and you will receive his approval, for he is God's servant for your good. But if you do wrong, be afraid, for he does not bear the sword in vain. For he is the servant of God, an avenger who carries out God's wrath on the wrongdoer. Therefore one must be in subjection, not only to avoid God's wrath but also for the sake of conscience. (Romans 13:1-7, ESV).

The passage teaches that if we do what is good, we can live without fearing those in authority, avoid God's wrath, and enjoy a clear conscience.

The most visible form of the government and its laws on a daily basis – for most folks – is the local police force. As an agent of the government, charged with the responsibility to serve and protect, Hoppy told his viewers the police officer was worthy of our respect. Hopalong's message to the kids in the episode trailer for the episodes, "The Renegade Press" and "The Outlaw's Reward" was:

> Hi, my little partners. I want to ask you a very serious question. Are you afraid of policemen? You're not, huh? Well, that's good! You shouldn't be! Always remember that those men have had a lot of training, and have put in a lot of years to learn how to help protect you. And one more thing – don't ever call a policeman a 'cop'! He doesn't like it and it doesn't sound good. Respect him as he does you. Call him a 'police officer' and see how much nicer he'll be. I'll see you next week. In the meantime, don't forget to go to Sunday School. (Trailer #12, *Hopalong Cassidy* television series).

The reminder to attend Sunday School is interesting in this context, since – whether intended here or not – it invokes the idea that we are all also subject to the laws of a higher authority. As noted above in the passage in Romans 13, "there is no authority except from God, and those that exist have been instituted by God."

10. Children in many foreign lands are less fortunate than you. Be glad and proud you are an American.

The theme of patriotism was also common among the creeds and codes of TV's western heroes. Freedom of speech, freedom of religion, and freedom to pursue life, liberty and happiness were among the ideals championed by the cowboys of the small screen. Hopalong Cassidy represented these themes well, both on screen and off. For example, consider freedom of religion. Two different episode trailers ended with the reminder for kids and their families to enjoy their right to worship freely in this country. Hoppy ended the trailer for episodes, "The Renegade Press" and "The Outlaw's Reward," with the words: "I'll see you next week. In the meantime, don't forget to go to Sunday School." Similarly, the salutation in the trailer for episodes, "Copper Hills" and "Grubstake," was Hoppy's reminder: ". . . Now so long until next week - and in the meantime, don't forget to go to Sunday School."

The early-series episode, "The Marauders," contained a scene in which Hopalong, and sidekicks, Lucky and California, pull up their horses in front of a rural church in the evening of a day spent on the trail. Hoppy announces, "This looks like a good place for us to stop."

Lucky, apparently surprised by Hoppy's words, says: "But that's a church!"

Hopalong responds: "Well, what about it? It's not a bad place to spend a little time once in a while."

Patriotism, in the sense of being a good neighbor and respecting those among whom one resides, is certainly taught in the Bible. This type of patriotism is captured in Jesus' teachings – such as in the Golden Rule, and in various parables – and in verses like I Peter 2:17 (ESV), which instruct Christians to: "Honor everyone. Love the brotherhood. Fear God. Honor the emperor." Jesus also reminded his followers they were responsible to pay their taxes: "He said to them, 'Then render to Caesar the things that are Caesar's, and to God the things that are God's.'" (Luke 20:25, ESV).

With a quick internet search one can easily find plenty of Bible verses that call on us to be thankful for whatever blessings we enjoy. Christians were reminded in James 1:17 (KJV) that "every good gift and every perfect gift is from above," and in the early 1950s, people were aware of how good life in America was compared to many other nations around the world, including European nations that were still struggling to recover from the devastations of World War Two. We can better appreciate what we have by being mindful that there is always someone somewhere who must get by with less than we have.

In the episode trailer used at the close of episodes "The Valley Raiders" and "Frontier Law," Hoppy reinforced this article of his creed. These trailers were inserted before the closing credits, but after the sponsor's spot that followed the end of the story. Thus, in essence, this episode trailer underscored the economic liberty – and other freedoms – enjoyed by Americans:

Hi there! Did you hear what the man said? I did - and I agree with every word of it. If you buy his product, I'm sure you'll like it – and it'll tickle my sponsor to death. Now a thought for my little partners... be happy and proud that you're an American. Remember, there are millions of little boys and girls all over the world that would give anything for that privilege. Now, until next week, so long – and good luck to you! (Trailer #2, *Hopalong Cassidy* television series).

William "Hopalong Cassidy" Boyd in real life demonstrated his pride in being an American with his participation in various public events, such as parades. In a March, 1951 issue of *Television-Radio Mirror* magazine, he was also reported to have been a part of some *Voice of America* broadcasts. These broadcasts were part of an American international radio program series "designed to combat the spread of Communism by telling the truth about America."

A Role Model

William Boyd overwhelmingly succeeded in transforming Clarence Mulford's character of Hopalong Cassidy into a B western cowboy hero – first in film, then on radio and television. His "Creed for American Boys and Girls" set forth the ideals by which Hopalong Cassidy lived, and therefore, so should his young fans. The ten-point creed was a re-working of Hopalong's previously published eight-point Troopers Creed. The "Hopalong Cassidy Troopers Creed" included the following articles: .

To be kind to birds and animals
To always be truthful and fair
To keep your self clean and neat
To always be courteous
To be careful when crossing the streets
To avoid bad habits
To study and learn your lessons
To obey your parents.

Boyd revised the Troopers Creed into the ten-point creed after Gene and Roy had published their ten-point creeds.

As mentioned earlier, being the first television cowboy hero had a huge impact on the youth in America. The "Hopalong Cassidy Troopers' Club" had by early 1950 already grown to some two million members in the western portion of the United States, according to a story in the June 12,

1950 issue of *LIFE* magazine ("Hopalong Hits the Jackpot", *LIFE*, June 12, 1950), which also featured William Boyd on the front cover as Hopalong Cassidy. The same magazine story reported that Boyd recognized his responsibility as a role model to the children watching him on television. In the article, Boyd is quoted: "The parents preach what a wonderful guy Hoppy is. What...do you do? You have to be a wonderful guy."

Promotional photo of Hopalong Cassidy.

Hopalong Cassidy's Creed

For American Boys and Girls

1. The highest badge of honor a person can wear is honesty. Be truthful at all times.

2. Your parents are the best friends you have. Listen to them and obey their instructions.

3. If you want to be respected, you must respect others. Show good manners in every way.

4. Only through hard work and study can you succeed. Don't be lazy.

5. Your good deeds always come to light. So don't boast or be a show-off.

6. If you waste time or money today, you will regret it tomorrow. Practice thrift in all ways.

7. Many animals are good and loyal companions. Be friendly and kind to them.

8. A strong, healthy body is a precious gift. Be neat and clean.

9. Our country's laws are made for your protection. Observe them carefully.

10. Children in many foreign lands are less fortunate than you. Be glad and proud you are an American.

of Hoppy's fading popularity. But television was coming on with a rush and Boyd knew it. In August, 1948, the first Hopalong movie was shown on a TV screen. And within a year, Boyd was well on his way to becoming a national hero.

Today, the man who used to feel cramped in a 22-room mansion is content in a servantless, four-room bungalow atop the Hollywood hills. Here he lives a simple life with the woman he married soon after he started the Hopalong series. Grace Bradley, a beautiful blonde, is the ideal Mrs. Cassidy. As a schoolgirl

Hopalong Cassidy's Creed appeared in print in the December, 1950 issue of *Coronet*. The magazine article included an offer to readers to get their own copy suitable for framing!

Hoppy speaks directly to his television viewers in Trailer #9, telling his "little partners" that when their mother "asks you to do anything, don't fuss about it - just do it." (Trailer #9, used with *Hopalong Cassidy* episodes "The Emerald Saint," and "The Devil's Idol.")

In the comic book story, "The Land Grabbers," Hoppy demonstrated that his creed point, "If you want to be respected, you must respect others," applied regardless of one's ethnicity. (*Hopalong Cassidy*, April, 1950.)

5

THE LONE RANGER

OPENING CREDITS
With the classic music of the William Tell Overture playing in the background, the viewer hears:

> NARRATOR: The Lone Ranger!
> [gunshots are fired]
> THE LONE RANGER: Hi-yo, Silver!
> NARRATOR: A fiery horse with the speed of light, a cloud of dust and a hearty "Hi-yo Silver" - the Lone Ranger!
> THE LONE RANGER: Hi-yo, Silver, away!
> NARRATOR: With his faithful Indian companion, Tonto, the daring and resourceful masked rider of the plains led the fight for law and order in the early West. Return with us now to those thrilling days of yesteryear. The Lone Ranger rides again!

Who Was That Masked Man?

A man wearing a black mask…a silver bullet…the cry of "hi-yo, Silver"…the William Tell Overture – together or in any combination easily conjures up in one's mind the image of the Lone Ranger. Even one of those things individually can bring to mind the Lone Ranger, a testament of the unique and powerful image of this western hero decades removed from his introduction to the culture.

The story of the Lone Ranger has been told on radio, television, in movie serials, in comic strips and comic books, and, more recently, re-told in a Disney film. Author John Dunning asserted: "He is simply the best-known hero of the West ever created. On name recognition alone, he would chalk up more votes than Matt Dillon, Zorro, Red Ryder, and all the heroes of Zane Grey and Louis L'Amour combined." Dunning wrote that in 1998, and it still true today.

The character of the Lone Ranger had his beginning on Detroit's WXYZ radio station in 1933 as a three-times-a-week, fifteen-minute serial. The show quickly gained popularity, expanding into the Chicago and New York markets. Both the character and the show were created by George Trendle and Fran Striker, with Earl Grasser as the primary actor voicing the Lone Ranger during the early years, and the part of Silver handled by the studio sound-effects department. A 1943 article in *Radio Mirror* noted the show appealed to adults and children alike with a hero who "epitomizes the legendary triumph of right over wrong, of justice over injustice, in the days of the opening of the West."

From the beginning, the show was an action-packed adventure in which the Lone Ranger was known to appear out of nowhere when trouble came, always ready to fight for law and order, then disappeared mysteriously after the wrong had been made right. An additional layer of mystery was added by keeping the identity of the Lone Ranger a secret – even the actors who portrayed him on radio were never shown without his mask, according to a report in a September, 1938, issue of *Radio Mirror*. The same article attempted to explain why so many radio listeners were captured by the show:

> The main reason for the huge popularity of *The Lone Ranger* is that the story is all action, all hair-breadth escapes. Although scattered, halfhearted complaints have been made about its effect upon youthful fans, *The Lone Ranger* has none of the brutality or viciousness of gangster stories. Instead, it is a return to the refreshing out-of-door adventure of the old dime novels. (*Radio Mirror*, September, 1938).

These same aspects of the radio show – action-packed, narrow escapes – were later carried over into the television version of the show. Some of the television episodes contained in the DVD sets available today contain the narration used with the closing credits: "Be with the Lone Ranger and Tonto same time next week for new dangers in another thrill-packed adventure. The Lone Ranger rides again!'"

Following the tragic death of Earl Grasser in 1941, Brace Beemer became the voice of the Lone Ranger, and the show continued without missing a beat. By the middle of World War Two, the Lone Ranger had become a cultural icon. "Certainly no single figure on radio or screen has so captured the hearts and imagination of Americans as the Lone Ranger," reported an article in the August, 1943, issue of *Radio Guide*. The article further speculated that "To every American, the radio and screen dramas of the 'Lone Ranger,' founded as they are on the law of right living and plain justice, spell something of the spirit that makes America - the spirit and way of life that Americans are fighting to keep alive in a war-torn world."

The Lone Ranger had by this time become a well-known symbol of high ideals in the culture. By January of 1943, total membership in the Lone Ranger Safety Club was reportedly around 4,400,000 boys and girls. So popular was the character that the U.S. War Department enlisted his support for the war effort on the World War Two home front. The Lone Ranger asked his Safety Club members and their parents to keep buying war

The Lone Ranger appealed to adults as well as juveniles. A funny story about two elder fans of the show was reported at the time:
> The Lone Ranger almost landed two of his fans in jail the other day. An elderly couple, driving quietly and peaceably along a highway near San Francisco, suddenly speeded up and whizzed through a tunnel at sixty miles an hour. A motor cop stopped them and remonstrated—at which they explained that *The Lone Ranger* was on, the tunnel cut off reception on their car radio, and they had to hurry so they wouldn't miss too much of the action! . . . The cop let 'em go.

(*Radio Mirror*, December, 1938)

bonds and stamps and to plant victory gardens. In May, 1943, the New Jersey branch of the National Federation of Press Women named the *Lone Ranger* the best children's program on radio, citing the "valuable influence it has exerted in subtly instilling into youthful listeners' minds the principles of good citizenship, courage and high ideals."

Shortly after the end of the war, an estimated audience of more than ten million people were tuning in three times per week to listen to the adventures of the Lone Ranger on ABC radio (as reported in *Broadcasting,* May 17, 1948). Even after the television show was on the air, the Lone Ranger continued to be quite popular on the radio. As late as the 1954-1955 broadcast season, when the show was airing three times a week (Monday-Wednesday-Friday) during prime time, it was the winner of a *TV Radio Mirror* readers' poll for favorite children's program on radio (*TV Radio Mirror,* May, 1955).

After sixteen very successful years on radio, the owner of the Lone Ranger property, George W. Trendle, made a deal with the radio version's longtime sponsor, General Mills, to bring the Lone Ranger to television. The series premiered on the ABC television network on September 15, 1949, with Clayton Moore as the Lone Ranger. The Cisco Kid and the Lone Ranger were the first heroes of made-for-TV half-hour programs to appear on television. As discussed previously, Hoppy was the first western hero to appear on television, but did so by way of using edited versions of his movies.

The Lone Ranger was thus a contributing factor in the rapid rise in television sales and viewership across the country. When the show first went on the air in 1949, the estimated number of TV sets in existence was already 3,200,000. By the end of the following year, industrial surveys reported that about 18% of U.S. families owned TV sets. By early 1953, that estimate had grown to 44% of families (about 19.5 million households) having their own TV set, with the greatest concentration (by far) in the large (population greater than 500,000) Northeastern cities.

As popular as the radio show was in the late 1940s, the television version of the show turned the Lone Ranger into a true American icon, with Clayton Moore becoming identified with the character in the same manner as William Boyd had become Hopalong Cassidy. Clayton Moore had been chosen to play the character in part because General Mills wanted to protect their investment on the radio side. Television in 1949 was still seen as an experiment in a fledgling industry, and the sponsor apparently did not want to risk the radio program's success by a potential failure on the television side. It turned out, of course, that there was no need to worry. Almost immediately, the show was recognized as a success, with an industry trade magazine noting that, along with *Captain Video*, the *Lone Ranger* was an early hit as an adventure show aimed at kids, with sponsors enjoying greater brand recognition and much higher sales generation than ever experienced with radio (*Sponsor*, Sept 26, 1949).

By June, 1950, *Sponsor* magazine was reporting the top film favorites on TV included *The Lone Ranger*, *Hopalong Cassidy*, and the *Cisco Kid*. For *The Lone Ranger*, TV and radio shows were both being produced and aired, while plenty of tie-in merchandising such as a comic strip, comic books, puzzles, guns, badges, masks, suits and other gadgets was selling in the millions. General Mills was the happy sponsor of a show placing in the top ten Nielsen TV ratings, with its filmed commercials used in the show to advertise such General Mills products as Cheerios, Bisquick, and Betty Crocker Cake Mixes. Adult interest in the show was sufficiently impressive that General Mills decided to re-run a series of episodes during the summer of 1950 for the late evening hours of 9:00 and 10:00 P.M. (*Sponsor*, September 25, 1950). *The Lone Ranger* was voted "Favorite TV western program" for 1950 by readers of *Television Radio Mirror*, as reported in their May, 1951 issue.

Clayton Moore starred in the television show as the Lone Ranger, with his sidekick, Tonto, played by Jay Silverheels. For a while, the Lone Ranger was played by John Hart, but Moore returned to the role in 1954 and remains the actor most associated with the character.

In 1958, the U.S. government again enlisted the services of the Lone Ranger to promote the sale of U.S. Savings Stamps among young people. At that time, the Lone Ranger's "Peace Patrol" was part of the most intensive campaign the Treasury Department had conducted since World War Two.

In the television series, the Lone Ranger and Tonto were always on the move throughout the West, helping right a wrong in one place before disappearing to show up in another place where their help was needed. The storylines and action sequences were similar to that seen in other B westerns on television at the time, in which the bad guys were usually involved in stagecoach robberies, cattle rustling, bank robberies, fraudulent land grabs, gold mine claim jumping, and other such criminal activity. Both the Lone Ranger and Tonto only used their guns to disarm the outlaws. As in *The Roy Rogers Show*, what would have been saloon scenes were usually cafes featuring waiters serving food rather than bartenders serving liquor. For example, in the episode, "The Beeler Gang," an outlaw enters a cafe, approaches the bar and orders a beer. He receives from the waiter only the immediate, curt reply, "No beer."

The Lone Ranger at times uses one of several disguises which allow him to work undercover. For example, he may appear as an Old-Timer, or the Swede, or show up as a Medicine Man. These situations tended to add a bit of humor in the story, as well, and, on rare occasions, Tonto would also work in disguise.

The iconic silver bullet served as the Lone Ranger's "calling card." The presentation of a silver bullet by someone meant they had been in contact with the Lone Ranger and were acting on his behalf. In the series' second episode, "The Lone Ranger Fights On," the Lone Ranger said the silver bullet was intended to be a symbol for "justice by law."

Overall, the Lone Ranger's character and mode of operation on television was simply a continuation of what had already been established on the radio program back in 1933. In an article in *TIME* magazine, the writer commented on the Lone Ranger's impeccable character: "Basically, the Ranger's five writers are guided by a short list of 'do's,' e.g., the Ranger always speaks good English, is always on the side of law & order, and a longer list of 'don'ts,' e.g., the Ranger never smokes, swears, drinks, shoots to kill, has love affairs, uses slang or does any wrong of any kind." (*TIME*, Jan 14, 1952). The same article quoted George Trendle about the ultimate goal with the character of the Lone Ranger: "Without detracting from the thrill and excitement, we try to convey a message that subtly teaches patriotism, tolerance, fairness and respect for the rights of all men."

The Lone Ranger was not your average cowboy-turned-lawman. He was seen to be a well-educated man, demonstrating at least a working knowledge of a wide range of subjects: the Bible, the works of Shakespeare, geography, Native American tribal customs, the laws of the land, human psychology, and much more. He could also speak a few words in a language other than English.

In addition to things like the mask and silver bullets, the Lone Ranger is also distinct from the other B western heroes by virtue of having a sidekick who was a Native American and a trusted, equal partner in their adventures. Thus, in every episode of the series, the two men were a perfect example of living out the first two items in the Lone Ranger Creed. Played perfectly by Jay Silverheels, Tonto always displayed intelligence and wisdom, and was shrewd in reaction to any mistreatment he experienced when he encountered racist people. The usual practice of Tonto was to follow the Lone Ranger's lead, but fortunately for the both of them, their individual strengths complemented each other so as to make them a formidable team in the fight for justice.

There were many times throughout the series in which Tonto is acting independently, as a hero in his own right. Whenever someone – man or animal – needed medical attention, it was typically Tonto who provided the appropriate treatment needed. On many occasions, Tonto acted on his own to rescue the Lone Ranger from a life-threatening situation. In at least one story, "Counterfeit Redskins," Tonto acts almost as the lone hero of the story, playing the lead role in resolving the conflict between two groups of people. Also, as witnessed in "The Banker's Son," Tonto took pride in being an equal partner with the Lone Ranger. In that story, the Lone Ranger is about to step into a fight to defend Tonto against a disreputable deputy, when Tonto stops him, saying, "No, Kemo Sabay, this my fight!" Tonto proceeds then to fight and knock out the deputy on his own.

One more thought on Tonto. Though some modern audiences may dislike the broken English Tonto uses in the show's dialogue, it should not be considered a demeaning trait. Rather, it served to highlight the fact that here was a man who could speak multiple languages! Not many Americans, in the 1950s or today even, can make such a claim.

John Dunning's summary of the radio show applies equally to the television version: "The show today retains its eternal airs: the virtues of purity were never better utilized."

Clayton Moore later wrote of the care given to protect the image – and thereby, the intended message – of the Lone Ranger: "… we were careful to be respectful to all people at all times. We never smoked when in costume. We showed respect for the police and the concepts of law and order. We always remembered that fair play and honesty were the most important qualities to get across to the kids." (Clayton and Thompson, *I Was That Masked Man*).

The Lone Ranger Creed

1. I believe that to have a friend, a man must be one;
2. That all men are created equal and that everyone has within himself the power to make this a better world;
3. That God put the firewood there, but that every man must gather and light it himself;
4. In being prepared physically, mentally, and morally to fight when necessary for that which is right;
5. That a man should make the most of what equipment he has;
6. That "this government, of the people, by the people, and for the people," shall live always;
7. That men should live by the rule of what is best for the greatest number;
8. That sooner or later...somewhere...somehow...we must settle with the world and make payment for what we have taken;
9. That all things change, but the truth, and the truth alone lives on forever;
10. I believe in my Creator, my country, my fellow man.

The Lone Ranger's creed was developed earlier during the radio years and appeared in print at least as early as 1943 in an issue of *Radio Guide*. It summarized the Lone Ranger's values by which both he and Tonto lived and worked, as seen consistently throughout the stories in the television series.

1. I believe that to have a friend, a man must be one.

When a stranger once asked the Lone Ranger point-blank, "Who's the Indian?", the Lone Ranger, without hesitation, answered simply, "He's my friend." That brief exchange happened early in the television series (in the third episode of the first season) and confirmed what the audience already knew about the bond of friendship between Tonto and the Lone Ranger. In the very first episode of *The Lone Ranger*, we learn this friendship actually began several years prior to the ambush of the Texas Rangers by the Cavendish gang. Apparently, when both men were still boys, the Lone Ranger had acted as a friend during a time of crisis to help Tonto. Thus, when the injured and left-for-dead Lone Ranger needed help, it was a friend from his past – Tonto – who came to his rescue.

In the Bible, there are several examples of strong friendships, such as that of David and Jonathan (see I Samuel 18:1-3, for example) and Ruth and Naomi (see Ruth 1:16-17). In Ecclesiastes 4:10 is found one of many verses dealing with the value of having good friends: "For if they fall, one will lift up his fellow. But woe to him who is alone when he falls and has not another to lift him up!" (Ecclesiastes 4:10, ESV). In the *Lone Ranger* episodes, the viewer sees examples of this often as either Tonto or the Lone Ranger rescue each other from perilous circumstances.

Extending kindness and being a friend in the spirit of the Golden Rule can be beneficial in a "pay it forward" manner, as seen in the *Lone Ranger* stories and in the Proverbs. In a season three episode, "El Toro," the Lone Ranger's nephew, Dan Reid, spared the life of an outlaw. At a critical point later in the story, that same outlaw acted to save the lives of Dan, Tonto and the Lone Ranger, because he felt indebted to them as a result of Dan's prior act of friendship. It is an illustration of the statement in Proverbs 29:5, "A man who flatters his neighbor spreads a net for his feet" (ESV).

Frequently throughout the series, we see the Lone Ranger and Tonto reconnecting with people they had previously befriended. Those already-existing relationships with Indian chiefs, sheriffs, marshals, ranchers, businessmen, and others, were always beneficial to the Lone Ranger as they were usually able to offer him information, food and shelter, or some other form of aid. In the second episode of the series, "The Lone Ranger Fights On," we learn that a trusted friend of the Lone Ranger – Jim Blane – knows the real identity of the Lone Ranger and will be depended upon to manage a secret silver mine near Colby in order to supply the Lone Ranger with bullets and money. Indeed, "a price can never be placed on friendship," the Lone Ranger stated in the episode, "The Bait: Gold."

2.   That all men are created equal and that everyone has within himself the power to make this a better world.

A common theme throughout the series was the restatement in various ways of the idea that all men are equal, and everyone can do something to make the world a better place to live. Late in the fourth season, in the episode "Code of the Pioneers," Dan Reid and the Lone Ranger are reading a letter from Tonto who is visiting in Washington, D.C. at the time. The Lone Ranger explains Tonto had been called to the capitol in order to receive an award, for which, according to Dan, Tonto is a deserving recipient: "He's done a lot to better the relations between the settlers and the Indians out here." Thus, Tonto is singled out as an example of one who treats others as equals and has personally worked to improve relations between different people groups.

This perspective that all men are created equal originates in the Bible. In Acts 17:26 (NASB) it is stated that God "made from one man every nation of mankind to live on all the face of the earth, having determined their appointed times and the boundaries of their habitation." Genesis 3:20 tells us that all humans have the same earthly mother, Eve – "she was the mother of all living."

In a late series episode, "Journey to San Carlos," the Lone Ranger and Tonto are seen discussing some of the distinctive cultural aspects of a local Indian tribe. A bit later in that story, a young white man is surprised when Tonto voluntarily risked his own life to save the young man and his sister: "Tonto, you'd risk your own life to save us? To save me? You, an Indian?"

Tonto responds, "All men are brothers, Mr. Walker. Some have red skin, some have black skin, some have white skin, but we all brothers."

Though not quoting from the Bible, Tonto's response certainly echoed scripture. In Malachi 2:10 (NASB), we are reminded of our common ancestry and the implied responsibility to treat one another in an honorable manner: "Do we not all have one father? Has not one God created us? Why do we deal treacherously each against his brother so as to profane the covenant of our fathers?"

When men fail to get along due to prejudice of any kind – due to race, gender, handicap, religious beliefs, etc., it leads to problems for everyone. As the Lone Ranger pointed out at the end of the story in "Trouble at Tylerville," an episode that had almost an "adult western" feel to it: "...I think you can see now what sort of disease intolerance really is – a sickness that hurts the persecutor as badly as the persecuted."

The influence of adults – positive or negative – on children is addressed in the episode, "The Letter Bride." The plot in this episode centers on the friendship between the Lone Ranger and Tonto and their Chinese friends. The Lone Ranger observed that "...children have no prejudice. I've seen them at play - yellow, red, black and white. They don't know there is any difference. They have to be taught prejudice by their elders or by people who can only feel big by making others feel small." Admiring the work ethic of the Chinese immigrants, the Lone Ranger stated the answer to the problem of racial prejudice in a community is "to fight it – it's the 'American Way'!" At the end of the episode, he again stated unequivocally that "there's no room in this country for racial prejudice. It just doesn't belong."

The Bible gives a New Testament example of a man – Peter – who was prejudiced against including Gentiles in the newly-established church. However, after a vision from God, Peter changed his thinking, and testified, "I most certainly understand now that God is not one to show partiality, but in every nation the man who fears Him and does what is right is welcome to Him."(Acts 10:34-35, NASB). Ethnicity does not matter; "race" does not matter. All humans have equal value and access to God.

This creed item also includes the idea that everyone has within them the power to make the world a better place in which to live – even those who may think they have nothing to offer the world. In "The Silent Voice," the Lone Ranger is able to communicate with a woman who is paralyzed and unable to use her voice by having her answer questions by simply blinking her eyes as a signal for 'yes' or 'no.' While local leaders had assumed the woman was rather useless, the Lone Ranger proved otherwise as she soon became the key to catching the outlaw in the story.

In the Old Testament, we have many examples of individual courage in action. Among them is the account of a woman who was encouraged to step into a position of great responsibility with the wise counsel of her uncle, who advised that perhaps God had placed her in that moment in history "…for such a time as this." That woman was Esther, chosen from among the population to be a queen.

The New Testament makes it clear that in Christ, we are all indeed brothers: "Here there is not Greek and Jew, circumcised and uncircumcised, barbarian, Scythian, slave, free; but Christ is all, and in all." (Colossians 3:11 ESV). As such, we have a responsibility to treat each other according to the Golden Rule. In that spirit, the Lone Ranger once counseled a man about how to approach pending negotiations with nearby Native Americans, telling him, "Not only must the Indians learn to deal fairly with the settlers, but we in return must learn to be fair and honest with them."

3. That God put the firewood there, but that every man must gather and light it himself.

A common theme voiced by the Lone Ranger throughout the series was the theme of economic progress through individual effort. He frequently spoke of the need for the wise use of natural resources and the role of both citizens and the government in the lawful expansion of business enterprises and development of the land. For example, in "The Old Cowboy," the Lone Ranger argues in favor of the railroad expanding into new areas of the West. Such expansion would provide new ways for typical farmers and ranchers to quickly move their products to market, and would bring jobs for other workers – a great opportunity for those who would be migrating from other places. In general, stated the Lone Ranger, it meant the West will prosper.

This creed item stressed the importance of the wise use of our natural resources, along with a recognition that work and individual effort would be required. As noted in previous chapters, the Bible teaches the value and rewards of honest labor. Proverbs 10:4 (ESV) states that "a slack hand causes poverty, but the hand of the diligent makes rich." The primary purpose of one's hard work is to provide for the welfare of his household. In I Timothy 5:8 (ESV), New Testament believers were reminded that "if anyone does not provide for his relatives, and especially for members of his household, he has denied the faith and is worse than an unbeliever." Again, in I Thessalonians 4:10-12 (ESV), the Christians were instructed to "aspire to live quietly, and to mind your own affairs, and to work with your hands," and in so doing, they would not be dependent on others.

Various episodic storylines also expressed the necessity of education as preparation for accomplishing the goals of this creed point. "Education is going to play a vital part in the growing of the West," stated the Lone Ranger as he contributed his share of an estate to the endowment of a mining college (in "Gold Town"). In several of the episodes in which the Lone Ranger's nephew Dan Reid appears it is stated that the young man is currently pursuing a college degree. In Proverbs 18:15, we read "the heart of the prudent getteth knowledge; and the ear of the wise seeketh knowledge" (KJV).

In the episode, "White Hawk's Decision," Little Hawk has just returned to the West after attending and graduating from a college in the East, and upon meeting the Lone Ranger, tells him he is "carrying nothing more valuable than a little knowledge." The Lone Ranger adds, "which is worth more than gold – and more difficult to steal." Perhaps the Lone Ranger was thinking of the words in Proverbs 16:16 (ESV): "How much better to get wisdom than gold! To get understanding is to be chosen rather than silver." The Little Hawk character was returning to his people ready to apply his education as a leader in the area of agriculture for the purpose of helping his people be economically independent.

When each individual puts forth the effort in work and study, not only will they benefit, but so will the society in which they live and work. This was the lesson in the episode, "The Map." At the end of the action, the Lone Ranger tells a young boy who had already demonstrated an interest in chemistry to "keep up the good work, Buddy. The West needs boys like you who want to build things, instead of men like these who merely want to tear things down." A bit later, he added, "I wish you could invent a powder, Buddy, that would make people realize the importance of progress and mutual trust and cooperation. But I guess that's something that each man has to learn for himself."

4. In being prepared physically, mentally, and morally to fight when necessary for that which is right.

If there is any single creed article the average viewer may choose when describing the Lone Ranger's actions, it may well be this one. The Lone Ranger and Tonto were always seen as ready to fight on behalf of someone being wronged. The key to their getting involved was whether the fight was "necessary" and "for that which is right." In the first episode of the second season ("Million Dollar Wallpaper"), two old-timers are attempting to have a duel to settle an argument. The Lone Ranger and Tonto interrupt them, and the Lone Ranger comments, "anyone who tries to settle an argument by fighting is silly."

In "The Tenderfeet," the Lone Ranger assured the local sheriff, "I never interfere with the law unless it promises a breach of justice." However, the Lone Ranger was willing to get involved in a fight whenever fighting was necessary to support a just cause. In Proverbs 31:8-9 (ESV), we read, "Open your mouth for the mute, for the rights of all who are destitute. Open your mouth, judge righteously, defend the rights of the poor and needy." Also, in Psalm 82:3 (ESV), we again see the instruction to fight for a just cause: "Give justice to the weak and the fatherless; maintain the right of the afflicted and the destitute."

When the cause was a just cause and a need to fight for the cause existed, the Lone Ranger was always prepared to take quick and decisive action. A new rancher was worried about their chances of standing up to an outlaw gang known to be a group of tough fighters in "Rustler's Hideout," but the Lone Ranger assured him, "We can be tough, too, Fred – when we have to be!" At the end of the story in "The Brown Pony," young Tommy tells Tonto, "The Lone Ranger told me I can never solve a problem by running away from it."

The idea of being prepared – physically, mentally, and morally – surfaces in scriptures like Isaiah 1:17 (ESV), which states: "Learn to do good; seek justice, correct oppression; bring justice to the fatherless, plead the widow's cause." Being prepared involves "learning" on multiple levels: physical, mental and moral. The Lone Ranger was physically prepared, as seen in "White Hawk's Decision," when a young Indian boy, Arrowfoot, admired how the Lone Ranger could do fancy trick shots with his pistols. Arrowfoot said it was "truly magic," but the Lone Ranger corrected him: "Not magic, Arrowfoot. Practice. Aim. Control." Mental preparation includes the ability to think independently and make rational decisions. The Lone Ranger once lectured an army lieutenant: "Let me remind you once again. A good officer is one who can adapt himself to new situations, without the aid of a rule book!" (in "Jornada Del Muerto"). Moral preparation includes the necessity of honesty and integrity of character for those who would fight for a good cause. For example, in "Sheriff's Sale," a man's reputation for honesty is how the Lone Ranger knew that man was innocent: "We knew you'd been framed because we knew you wouldn't accept a bribe." He noted the sheriff had set a good example for others in the community.

Concluding the story in "Sheriff's Sale," the Lone Ranger makes the point that "No matter how many sheriffs, policemen, marshals a community may have, real law enforcement depends upon the courage and integrity of every individual citizen." This statement is consistent with the summary statement in Micah 6:8 about what God expects from each of us in this life: "He has told you, O man, what is good; and what does the Lord require of you but to do justice, and to love kindness, and to walk humbly with your God?" (Micah 6:8, ESV). In the New Testament, we read a similar characterization of a righteous life: "Religion that is pure and undefiled before God, the Father, is this: to visit orphans and widows in their affliction, and to keep oneself unstained from the world." (James 1:27 ESV).

Every man faces a challenge sooner or later in life, but it is his reaction to those challenges that counts, according to the Lone Ranger in "Quarter Horse War." When faced with a challenge, "You either face that challenge, or you run away from it. . . . You're only a failure if you admit it. A man can go down, but if he goes down fighting he's a success – at least, he's tried!"

In the narration before the closing credits of many early series episodes, the viewer was reminded of the centrality of this creed item to the Lone Ranger's actions: "Will the Lone Ranger triumph as he fights on for justice, law, and order? Be sure to be with us again next week at this same time, when General Mills brings you another thrilling adventure with the Lone Ranger!"

5.   That a man should make the most of what equipment he has.

For the purpose of this discussion, "equipment," can be represented in the form of material assets, tools, or talents, and could be considered as gifts provided by God, which, according to I Peter 4:10 (ESV), should be used "to serve one another, as good stewards of God's varied grace." Interestingly, the Lone Ranger apparently was in the practice of putting aside cash for personal savings, since in the episode "Two for Juan Ringo" it is revealed that he had a personal bank account and personally knew the banker. This implicitly informed young viewers that the Lone Ranger was responsible with the care of his money.

This creed item would seem most directly to communicate the value of putting to good use one's equipment at hand, rather than making excuses while accomplishing little or nothing. There were numerous times in which the Lone Ranger and Tonto made use of whatever they could get their hands on that would help them escape a dangerous situation. For example, in "Million Dollar Wallpaper," the Lone Ranger took apart the handle of his pistol in order to use it as a wrench and free himself and the old-timer from the room in which they had been locked. On a couple of other occasions, the Lone Ranger used invisible ink and disappearing ink as a means to catch an outlaw. Of course, there were also many times where the Lone Ranger is seen in disguise working undercover to help solve a mystery.

A person is also responsible for the proper care of their own equipment. In the New Testament, it is stated that "it is required of stewards that they be found trustworthy." (I Corinthians 4:2 ESV). Again, with the definition of equipment as that which a person has or owns in order to do their work, the Lone Ranger and Tonto had two highly-valued assets in their horses – Silver and Scout. In the story, "Gold Train," a character named Horseface Jackson admires Silver, who at the time was standing at the hitching rail, and observed that "you can always tell a good man by the way he treats his horse." A little later, Jackson told Tonto, "You can always tell the character of a man by the horse he rides."

The Lone Ranger and Tonto were always traveling on horseback throughout the country, but they knew how to use what little equipment they had in a way that would be helpful to others.

6. That "this government, of the people, by the people, and for the people," shall live always.

In the episode, "Bullets for Ballots," the Lone Ranger and Tonto are concerned about whether a pending election in a small town will be conducted properly. "The right to vote is one of our most precious privileges and too often it's misused. Any election – even a small one like this – can be very important," stated the Lone Ranger.

Later in the story when a mayoral candidate is holding at gunpoint the Lone Ranger and Tonto (because he thinks they are outlaws), Tonto says, "Man who use force instead of good reason, not make good mayor."

At the end, when the good guy, Bob McQueen, has won the election, the Lone Ranger reminds him: "Bob, you do owe the people a good government."

This creed item recognizes the American system of government as a democratic form of government designed to be formed and maintained by its citizens for the general welfare and prosperity of its citizens. The *Lone Ranger* stories frequently involve the Lone Ranger's concern for the continued development of the West and the corresponding role of government to protect its citizens' personal liberties and private property rights.

A couple of Bible passages will suffice to show that governmental authority is derived from God and that a nation's peoples are instructed to be cooperative with that authority. Colossians 1:16 (ESV) states the origin of human government: "For by him all things were created, in heaven and on earth, visible and invisible, whether thrones or dominions or rulers or authorities—all things were created through him and for him." Then in the book of Titus, we see a description of what a good citizen looks like (that reads like something the Lone Ranger himself would have written): "Remind them to be submissive to rulers and authorities, to be obedient, to be ready for every good work, to speak evil of no one, to avoid quarreling, to be gentle, and to show perfect courtesy toward all people." (Titus 3:1-2, ESV).

In many stories throughout the series, the Lone Ranger is seen fighting corruption in governmental offices that would threaten the free exercise of liberty. He gets involved in such causes as protecting the individual's right to vote in a fair election, defending the ownership of private property, and ensuring the unhindered operation of a free press. The Lone Ranger firmly believed in the right of citizens to own and use private property, as seen in "Outlaw's Trail." After the Lone Ranger and Tonto had intervened to foster peaceful relations and cooperation among the farmers and ranchers in a Western community, the Lone Ranger summarized: "Everyone's entitled to his own way of life. Confirm the right of man to own property and to do with it as he chooses, and you'll give your children a real heritage!"

In many other stories, the Lone Ranger wants citizens to view their government favorably, with a confidence that their rights and property are secure. To that end, the Lone Ranger pursues outlaws whose actions would undermine that confidence. For example, in "Thieves' Money," the Lone Ranger is attempting to capture outlaws involved in counterfeit operations because, "Counterfeit money can do as much damage as the most vicious outlaw gang."

In another episode, "The Black Widow," a prisoner was released after serving time in a Federal prison for robbing a military payroll. Tonto, referring to the prisoner, commented: "Him steal from United States - that plenty bad."

To this, the Lone Ranger replied: "Yes, Tonto. When a man cheats and robs the United States' government, he robs every man, woman, and child in America. It's a crime against all of us."

The theme of America being founded on the principle of equal opportunity for all of its citizens was hit upon in a late series episode titled, "The Prince of Buffalo Gap," in which a prince from a foreign county visited the United States. At the end of the story, the prince said that the

Lone Ranger and Tonto taught him that it is not important what title a man may claim, but that a man's character is actually what counts in life.

7. That men should live by the rule of what is best for the greatest number.

Humans are naturally selfish (consider how readily a toddler first learns to use the word "mine!"). Yet, to live life in a selfless manner is a regular teaching found in the Bible. Jesus instructed his followers to "love your neighbor as yourself" (Mark 12:31, NLT), and we know from Jesus' parable of the Good Samaritan that "your neighbor" is virtually anyone with whom you have personal contact. Living in a selfless manner is also a logical way to improve one's life, as noted in Proverbs 18:1 (NLT), "Unfriendly people care only about themselves; they lash out at common sense."

In the story in "Sunstroke Mesa," the Lone Ranger and Tonto seek to recover stolen donations that were intended to fund an irrigation project. They were concerned that without the irrigation project being completed, the farmers would have been ruined financially during the next planting season. The story was one of many examples where the Lone Ranger is not just helping one individual or family, but working for the welfare of an entire community in the spirit of this creed article and consistent with the instruction in this New Testament passage: "Do nothing from selfishness or empty conceit, but with humility of mind regard one another as more important than yourselves; do not merely look out for your own personal interests, but also for the interests of others." (Philippians 2:3-4, NASB).

Living in a selfless manner, ready to serve others, is a common theme in scripture and is commonly portrayed in the stories of the Lone Ranger. In 2 Thessalonians 3:13 (ESV) is a reminder to "not grow weary in doing good." A specific example is given in the Old Testament in Deuteronomy 22:4 (ESV): "You shall not see your brother's donkey or his ox fallen down by the way and ignore them. You shall help him to lift them up again." The Lone Ranger once dealt with a sheriff who, like many people, had ignored known problems around him simply because he did not think he was personally affected (in "Behind the Law") by those problems.

In another New Testament verse, early Christians were taught they must "…learn to devote themselves to good works, so as to help cases of urgent need, and not be unfruitful." (Titus 3:14, ESV). Everyone benefits when all of us live by the rule of doing what is good and right, as embodied in the

Golden Rule. The Lone Ranger, in "The Twisted Track," was dealing with two ex-Confederate soldiers who were still bitter about their war experiences. The Lone Ranger spent time with the younger of the two, showing him how the people in the area had put their past behind them to work together for their common good. The Lone Ranger explained to him: "It's the same everywhere, Clint. Hatred and bitterness brought tragedy to this land. But now, with God's help, good will, and tolerance are repairing the damages. Those farms were made by good neighbors – Yanks, Rebs – working together for the good of all. It's the only way, Clint. Believe me."

8. That sooner or later...somewhere...somehow...we must settle with the world and make payment for what we have taken.

We will consider two applications of this creed article seen in the TV series: environmental responsibility, and moral accountability. An application with regard to the care of the natural environment and its resources would be a nod to scriptural passages like that found in Psalm 104:24-30, which acknowledges all of creation as a wonder-filled work of God for the benefit of all living creatures. However, man has been given an awesome responsibility for its care, as seen in Genesis 1:28. In this verse, God gives man "dominion over the fish of the sea and over the birds of the heavens and over every living thing that moves on the earth." (Genesis 1:28, ESV). The word "dominion" is used here in the sense of a caretaker or superintendent. Other passages in the Bible also address proper care of the earth's land and natural resources – see, for example, Ezekiel 34:17-18 and Leviticus 25:3-5.

It is noteworthy that throughout the entirety of *The Lone Ranger* series, the Lone Ranger and Tonto always take care to set up their campfires in a proper and safe manner. Every time they leave their campsite, they are seen taking a few seconds to properly extinguish their fire. They are seen doing this even at times when they are leaving in an urgent manner. The Lone Ranger and Tonto served as good role models for behavior that contributes to the preservation of our natural resources.

An application of this creed point with regard to morals or ethics is an easy and straight-forward reading of the statement. The Lone Ranger, in "Crime in Time," stated that criminals know that sooner or later their crimes will catch up with them. This was more or less the underlying theme of all the *Lone Ranger* stories.

In the episode titled, "The Lost Chalice," the Lone Ranger and Tonto develop a plan to help out farmers who are struggling in drought conditions. While in pursuit of a gang of thieves, a map is found, on which is written the references to a couple of Bible verses. At the conclusion of the story, one of those verses, Proverbs 26:27, is explained by the local Padre: "The most prophetic one of all, I think. 'He that diggeth a pit shall fall into it.' And that is exactly what happened to the three thieves – thanks to the Lone Ranger!"

This creed article, and many *Lone Ranger* storylines, reminded the viewer that all actions have consequences. The Lone Ranger reminded a hateful woman in "The Law and Miss Aggie" of the Biblical statement, "For they have sown the wind, and they shall reap the whirlwind." (Hosea 8:7, KJV). Our actions have consequences that are sometimes foreseeable, and may also be more overwhelming in nature than anticipated. In the Old Testament, Moses once advised the people if they failed on their promise, "your sin will find you out." (Numbers 32:23, KJV). In other words, the sin one commits will one day haunt them in such forms as misery, regret, bitterness, guilt and resentment.

In the episode, "The Cross of Santo Domingo," a man was caught stealing precious stones in order to sell them and use the money to pay for his invalid son's medical treatments. This episode taught the young viewers that the "ends do not justify the means" – even when the "cause" is a "good" one, stealing is wrong. At the end of the story, the Lone Ranger reminded everyone, "When a man breaks the law, he must pay his debt to society."

9.   That all things change, but the truth, and the truth alone lives on forever.

In the television series, the Lone Ranger is on a long crusade against injustice wherever he encounters it, dealing with such vices as greed, gambling, pride, deceitfulness, personal prejudices, and other "sins." The underlying or foundational thought in the Lone Ranger's mind is the reality of the existence of objective truth – an absolute standard of morality. As a distressed girl in "The Masked Rider" was reminded by the Lone Ranger, we cannot just make up the rules as we go; one's actions and behavior must be governed by truth.

As much as the Lone Ranger fought for law and order, and held in esteem the laws of the community, there was a higher goal of seeking the truth in any matter. This was the central lesson learned by the sheriff in the episode, "Tumblerock Law." In the story, Sheriff Brooks learned that while the enforcement of a law is important, one must get to the truth of the matter in order for justice to be served. At the end of the episode, he summarized his thoughts for the viewer: "You know, I learned quite a lot myself today. I found out there was something a good deal more important than the law – and that's justice. Examining the facts, and listening to both sides. I've made plenty of mistakes, but that won't happen again – thanks to the masked man."

In life, there are many things that are temporary or seasonal in nature. As noted in Ecclesiastes 3:1-2 (NASB), "There is an appointed time for everything. And there is a time for every event under heaven – a time to give birth and a time to die; a time to plant and a time to uproot what is planted." On the other hand, there are eternal truths to which all are subject. The Bible speaks of God as being the ultimate source of truth. For example, in Psalms 119:160 (KJV), we read: "Thy word is true from the beginning: and every one of thy righteous judgments endureth for ever." Later, the prophet Isaiah wrote "The grass withers, the flower fades, but the word of our God will stand forever." (Isaiah 40:8, ESV).

Even without the opportunity to read the Bible, God's laws (or truths) are part of our innate sense of what is right and wrong (see Romans 2:13-15). Perhaps the Lone Ranger was thinking this when he once lectured a young robbery suspect on the subject of conscience: "Don't you know that if you committed that robbery, you'll never be entirely free from questions again? Perhaps they'll come from the law, or perhaps they'll come from men like me. Worst of all they'll come from your own conscience. You'll never be able to escape them." (from the episode, "The Tell-Tale Bullet").

> "The western is in the soul of all Americans. It's our myth and our foundation. You have to believe in the purity of truth, that truth wins out, that if you are bad you might get your way again and again, but in the end truth wins."
>
> (Lorne Greene, as quoted in the article "Disney Productions Revives the Western", by Joan Hanauer, *Chicago Tribune*, March 17, 1985)

In some situations, the Lone Ranger directly appealed to the Bible as the authoritative source for a description of right or wrong behavior. In "The Avenger," the Lone Ranger helped a local officer of the law avoid a costly mistake by reminding him that his father had taught him to "judge not, that you be not judged" – a reference to Jesus' words in Matthew 7:1 (ESV). On another occasion, a father was quoting a Bible verse to self-justify his poor treatment of his son (in the episode, "A Message from Abe"). The Lone Ranger gave the father something to think about by responding with a quote from another scripture - "the love of money is a root of all kinds of evils" (I Timothy 6:10, ESV).

The Lone Ranger made no secret of the fact that the justice for which he fought was based on the existence of a higher law and eternal truth. Given the continuing popularity of westerns in video format during the 1950s, many book and magazine writers noted the fact that westerns included moral values that were common to and understood by all cultures. For example, in an article written for an industry publication in 1957, a psychologist wrote of westerns and western heroes:

A sophisticated world laughs at the knight in shining armor riding on a white horse. Nevertheless, something deep within us responds to pure heroism. One might almost compare the western with the morality plays developed in many lands. In the morality play, pure virtue is extolled and some of this virtue rubs off on an audience waiting to be reminded that these are the only worthwhile and eternal moral values. (*Broadcasting*Telecasting*, September 2, 1957).

The Lone Ranger himself believed in the value of telling stories to the young in which such heroes were presented as individuals pursuing truth and honor. In the episode, "Drink of Water," a father explains that he and his wife have told their young sons stories about heroes like Daniel Boone, Davy Crockett, and...the Lone Ranger. The Lone Ranger humbly tells the father that he hopes he can live up to the high standards the boy expects of him. Tonto is confident the Lone Ranger will not let the boy down. The Lone Ranger feels a great sense of responsibility as a role model, stating: "If Jackie believes in what I stand for, then when he grows up he'll fight for the same things that I do."

10. I believe in my Creator, my country, my fellow man.

This creed item seems to closely parallel the scripture in I Peter 2:17, in which readers are commanded: "Honor all people, love the brotherhood, fear God, honor the king." (I Peter 2:17, NASB) For convenience, we will look at each element – my Creator, my country, my fellow man – in turn.

"...my Creator"

This creed item specifies a belief in God, our Creator – a belief that is observable in various episodes of *The Lone Ranger*. The Bible presents a God who not only exists, but is also interested and involved in the lives of individual humans. In Psalm 14:1-4 (ESV), God is described as actively seeking – even among evildoers – those who are desiring to know Him: "The Lord looks down from heaven on the children of man, to see if there are any who understand, who seek after God." In Jeremiah 29:13 (ESV), God promised to be found by the honest seeker: "You will seek me and find me, when you seek me with all your heart." The New Testament passage written by Paul in Romans 1 explains that even for those without the benefit of the Hebrew scriptures, God was intentional in making himself visible to His creation (see Romans 1:20).

In some *Lone Ranger* stories, the viewer witnesses the acknowledgement of our human dependence upon God. For example, in "The Lost Chalice," a map is discovered upon which has been written the Bible references of Proverbs 26:27 and Psalms 121:1. From memory, the Lone Ranger quotes: "Psalms 121, verse 1 - I know that, Jose. 'I will lift up mine eyes unto the hills from whence cometh my help.'" In another episode, the Lone Ranger's nephew, Dan Reid, is in a desperate situation along with a young outlaw, Johnny. Left tied up under a blazing sun, Johnny wonders aloud if there is any hope for them or anything they could do to help themselves. Dan says there is something they can do – they can pray. He then bows his head in silent prayer for help. These scenes reveal a belief in the Creator, as noted in this creed item.

The story in the episode, "The Godless Men," appears to capture the essence of this creed point – that

"And without faith it is impossible to please him, for whoever would draw near to God must believe that he exists and that he rewards those who seek him."

(Hebrews 11:6, ESV)

God exists and cares for the individual – quite well. In this one story, the Lone Ranger: demonstrates a considerable knowledge about the function of the church in society; reveals a working knowledge of Biblical passages; and acknowledges the importance of freedom of religion.

The story begins when some outlaws rob a preacher in a hold up, stealing funds meant for the building of a church in Gold City. The preacher, the Reverend Randy Roberts, reluctantly hands over the money, telling the outlaws: "That money belongs to the Lord and His wrath is mighty!"

The outlaws' response includes the mention of the 8th Commandment, "thou shalt not steal," thus admitting they know they are guilty of doing wrong. The outlaws are connected with various Gold City businesses that involve owning and operating gambling houses, dance halls, and saloons. They are concerned about the downturn in profits that could result from the permanent presence of a preacher and a local church that would influence "god-fearing" people away from such businesses.

Upon first meeting the Lone Ranger, Rev. Roberts was not deterred by the Lone Ranger's mask: "I don't judge men by what's on their faces. I judge them by what's in their hearts. And I see nothing bad in yours." The Lone Ranger is happy to join forces with him in the fight against evil, saying he admires the courage, spirit, and fine reputation of the circuit-riding minister.

At the end of the story, the Lone Ranger has helped the Rev. Roberts get set up to publish the next issue of the local newspaper because he believes both freedom of the press and freedom of religion are equally important. The Rev. Roberts is then seen thinking aloud as he begins to write an editorial: "Citizens of Gold City: The godless men tried to destroy us, but the Lord did not desert us in our hour of need. He sent us a man whose name has always struck terror in the hearts of outlaws, a man whose valorous deeds are legion, whose courage is unsurpassed. We shall never forget the name of that man. He's the Lone Ranger."

"…my country"

The Lone Ranger was very much the patriot, as seen throughout the series and witnessed by fans in many personal appearances. The Lone Ranger and Tonto were seen in a late-series episode riding along slowly as the Lone Ranger admired the landscape around them. When Tonto finally inquired about what the Lone Ranger had been quietly contemplating, the

Lone Ranger said: "Tonto, I've been enjoying the country – thinking how lucky we are to be here. It's a great heritage, isn't it? Makes you realize how the poet felt when he wrote, 'I love thy rocks and rills, Thy woods and templed hills'" (he was quoting from what is now the lyrics for "My Country 'Tis of Thee," by Samuel Francis Smith).

The term patriot comes from the Greek root word pater, meaning father. A patriot can be generally defined as one who loves, supports and defends his fatherland, the country of his nativity or residence – with the emphasis on loving its people as an extended family of sorts, but not displaying an "exclusive superiority" mindset (which would be called nationalism or "a superpatriot"). There are several instances in the Bible in which people acted as patriots in this sense. Moses, for example, pleaded with God to spare his nation shortly after an act of rebellion against God, as recorded in Deuteronomy 9:6-29. Nehemiah, while serving in the court of a foreign power, prayed for his native land (see Nehemiah 1:4) and later risked his life to rebuild Jerusalem's walls and gates. Esther became a hero after she and Mordecai risked their personal safety to save their people. Daniel is another example of one who cared deeply for his people and prayed for the restoration of his nation (see Daniel 9:1-19).

A long, narrated introduction to the story in "The Renegades" covered a history of the westward expansion in United States, including the impact on Native Americans and the actions of the U.S. government during that expansion. This historical account is presented in a proud, patriotic manner, typical of the Lone Ranger's character in public appearances and other media. "I like to think of myself as an American who believes in the future of our Country, with its people living and working together," said the Lone Ranger in "One Nation Indivisible."

"…my fellow man"

Keeping in mind that Jesus defined our "neighbor" as being anyone with whom we have contact, the Bible – especially in the New Testament – commands that we honor and respect one another. "If you really fulfill the royal law according to the Scripture, 'You shall love your neighbor as yourself,' you are doing well." (James 2:8, ESV). Jesus had taught his disciples that the Golden Rule was central to the Old Testament law when he told them, "In everything, therefore, treat people the same way you want them to treat you, for this is the Law and the Prophets." (Matthew 7:12, NASB).

The old adage is that "actions speak louder than words," and the Lone Ranger and Tonto consistently demonstrated a love for their fellow man by their actions. As observed in numerous episodes, they were willing to partner with many people from many backgrounds, regardless of religion, ethnicity, gender or color. The Lone Ranger once remarked to a Catholic priest, "As you know, Padre, I have close friends in every religious faith, and I respect each of them equally" (from "The Lost Chalice"). In the episode, "A Broken Match," the story concludes with the banker's testimony of how he had been personally impacted by the Lone Ranger: "He not only recovered the bank's money, but he made me realize how wrong it is to judge a person on his past and not think of him by his hopes and ambitions for the future."

A Role Model

In one of the late-series episodes, "The Angel and the Outlaw," a lady known as "Mama Angel" and her adopted kids take in and care for Calico, a wounded outlaw for whom there is advertised a reward for his capture. The woman believes that according to the Bible's teachings, God expects her to provide care for the outlaw. "I wouldn't turn away a body that needs help," says Mama Angel. Hoping to convince Calico to mend his ways, she tells him, "If you're worth three thousand dollars as a bad man, you're worth a lot more as a good one."

Later, Mama Angel provides a meal for her kids, Calico, and the Lone Ranger (who is in disguise). Before eating, the young girl gives the blessing, thanking God for their food, and asking God's blessing and protection for them, plus help for Calico. However, the young boy, Manuel, has become infatuated with Calico – admiring him to the point of wanting to be just like him! The Lone Ranger reacts by appealing to Calico's conscience, asking him to undo some of the harmful influence Calico has had on Manuel – who had by then decided to abandon Mama Angel's counsel and become a famous outlaw like Calico. The Lone Ranger tells Mama Angel, "Someday he'll know it takes more than a gun and bad manners to be a brave man."

By the end of the story, Manuel realizes the outlaw life is not a good choice. As the Lone Ranger and Tonto ride away, Mama Angel tells Manuel, "That's a man you'd make no mistake in looking up to – that's the Lone Ranger!"

For millions of kids in the 1950s television audience, the Lone Ranger was just that – a man you could look up to. Clayton Moore took seriously this aspect of being the Lone Ranger. In his autobiography, *I Was That Masked Man*, he noted with regard to the Lone Ranger creed: "These good ideals were all a part of *The Lone Ranger*, but there was nothing preachy about the shows. They were fast paced, entertaining, and could be enjoyed by people of all ages. But I believe their enduring popularity stems from the character of the Lone Ranger himself."

In an episode titled, "Ghost Town Fury," the plot involved two boys who sneak away from home for an adventure in which they hope to be heroes like the Lone Ranger and Tonto. After being rescued from serious danger, they acknowledge they will not do such a foolish thing again. The Lone Ranger tells them, "I think you've both learned a good lesson – you should never go any place without first telling your parents!" It was yet another example of how parents could count on the Lone Ranger to be a good role model for their children.

Many adults can fondly recall enjoying watching *The Lone Ranger* on television as children, and for some, the wholesome influence of the show continued into their adult years. A fictional version of such was provided by the character in *Walker, Texas Ranger*, who became the sidekick to Chuck Norris' title character. In a scene within the first episode of that series, James Trivette told Cordell Walker of how he grew up in an urban environment in a Northeastern city, faithfully watching *The Lone Ranger* on Saturday morning television. From watching that show, Trivette said he was inspired to become a modern Texas Ranger.

In this regard, the Lone Ranger left a great legacy, as noted by Clayton Moore in the 1990s. "...I often meet adults in their thirties, forties, or fifties who, as soon as they recognize me, suddenly become six years old again. ...They remember the character and what he stood for." Moore elaborated:

To them, the Lone Ranger is more than a childhood hero. He's a reminder of a time when they were still optimistic, when they still believed in happy endings, knew that good would always win out. Maybe to those 'grown-up kids' the Lone Ranger is an ideal that means optimism is still possible, just like other 'outdated' ideas like integrity, generosity, bravery, and kindness. And maybe, because they still cherish these ideas, they're a little more likely to pass them on to their own kids. (Moore and Thompson, *I Was That Masked Man*).

Photo from back cover of Gold Key Giant comic, *The Lone Ranger Golden West*, October, 1966.

boy who said excitedly, "Gosh, Mom! Him and Silver look just the way they sound on the radio, don't they?" For the Lone Ranger stands six feet two inches, weighs two hundred pounds, and can ride anything that wranglers can saddle. He has blond hair, penetrating blue eyes, the slim waist of the westerner, and the broad shoulders of a long-distance swimmer. From spurs to sombrero, mask and six-shooters, small boys and girls from eight to eighty saw the exact materialization of their hero in real life.

Certainly no single figure on radio or screen has so captured the hearts and imagination of Americans as the Lone Ranger. To cliff-dwellers in the steel canyons of great cities, he stands for the romantic, adventure-filled West, described in stories they have read about the country that lies over the rim of their world, the places they dream of seeing one day. To the real westerner, who has wandered far from his native diggin's, the call of the Ranger and the beat of Silver's hoofs conjures a vivid picture of the Mesa with its background of ragged peaks that hood themselves in purple splendor at sunset. To every American, the radio and screen dramas of the "Lone Ranger," founded as they are on the law of right living and plain justice, spell something of the spirit that makes America—the spirit and way of life that Americans are fighting to keep alive in a war-torn world.

On January 23 of this year, when the "Lone Ranger" show celebrated its tenth anniversary on the airlanes, the National Safety Council bestowed a special award "for distinguished service to safety" on radioland's most famous ranger. At this time the total membership of the Lone Ranger Safety Club numbered 4,400,000 boys and girls. In his special powwow given during personal appearances at the circus, the Ranger asked members present to become American Rangers on the Home Front, to back our men on the fighting fronts. He urged them and their parents to buy more war bonds and stamps; plant victory gardens, adding, "Putting seeds in the ground means putting food into the mouths of our soldiers." He warned them, too, that loose talk can cost lives.

In May, the "Lone Ranger" series was again honored, this time by the New Jersey branch of the National Federation of Press Women. At a special-award ceremony the group named

never complain, just for the opportunity of seeing the Ranger and his famed steed.

BUT in the final analysis, it takes more than box-tops, excellent breakfast cereals, or even a man and his horse to make a radio and screen character the hero of boys and girls the world over. In the Lone Ranger's case, we believe that his creed of living has much to do with his fabulous popularity, especially in this last stronghold of freedom that is America. Here it is:

I BELIEVE . . .

—that to have a friend, a man must be one.

—that all men are created equal, and that everyone has within himself the power to help make this a better world.

—that God put the firewood there but every man must gather and light it himself.

—in being prepared physically, mentally and morally to fight when necessary for that which is right.

—that a man should make the most of what equipment he has.

—that "This Government of the people, by the people, and for the people" shall live always.

—that men should live by the rule of what is best for the greatest number.

—that sooner or later—somewhere, somehow—we must settle with the world and make payment for what we have taken.

—that all things change but truth and that truth alone lives on forever.

—in my Creator, my country, my fellow men.

(Signed) The Lone Ranger.

The "Lone Ranger" may be heard Mondays, Wednesdays and Fridays over the Blue Network at 7:30 p.m. EWT, 6:30 CWT, sponsored by General Mills for Korn-Kix, and in the South by American Bakeries. On the West Coast the "Lone Ranger" may be heard Mondays, Wednesdays and Fridays over the Don Lee Network at 7:30 p.m. PWT, 8:30 MWT, with sponsorship divided locally.

The Lone Ranger's creed appeared in an article published in the August, 1943, issue of *Radio Guide*.

Lassie and "Timmy" (Jon Provost) also joined The Lone Ranger's Peace Patrol! (*promotional photo from the author's collection*)

"Now, children," she said. "We'll try spelling. Does anyone know how to spell hero?"

"L-O-N-E R-A-N-G-E-R," said one boy.
"T-O-N-T-O," said a girl.
"You're both right," the teacher smiled.

The Lone Ranger and Tonto were both heroes, as seen in this story in Little Golden Book's, *The Lone Ranger and Tonto*.

Creeds, Codes and Cowboy Commandments

6

MORE COWBOYS AND CODES

While our focus has to this point been on the "big 4," Roy, Gene, Hoppy, and the Lone Ranger were not the only B western heroes to have a creed or code, nor were they the first. Some of the earliest movie cowboys were established role models for children well before television programming arrived on the scene. For example, Roy Rogers grew up a fan of movie cowboy Hoot Gibson. Clayton Moore, who played the Lone Ranger on television, recalled that as a child he wanted to be like such Western movie heroes as Tom Mix, Ken Maynard, and William S. Hart. In his autobiography, Moore described what those heroes meant to him:

> Those great Western stars were more to me than just good guys in a movie who rode beautiful horses and brought justice to the men in the black hats. They stood for something. I guess for lack of a better phrase I'd call it the American spirit. They were brave and fast on the draw, to be sure, but they also embodied ideas like justice and fair play and patriotism. That struck a deep chord in me. My dream was that someday I could be like them. (Moore and Thompson, *I Was That Masked Man*).

In this chapter, we will turn our attention to some other B western television heroes and their written creeds. Like the "big 4" already discussed, they were known on a national level. However, we will also briefly cover some of the very popular cowboy heroes who only appeared in their local television markets, but were known to have expressed their values in a membership pledge or with a set of club rules. First, though, we will take notice of a couple of pre-television cowboys.

Tom Mix

Many cite "The Great Train Robbery" as the first real feature film ever made. Released in 1903, it was a western movie that introduced the man who would become the first western movie hero, Broncho Billy Anderson. Thus was born the "western" and, as described in a 1959 article appearing in *TIME* magazine, it was "love at first sight" between Hollywood, the Wild West, and the movie-going public. Others soon appeared on the silver screen, including William S. Hart, Tom Mix, Buck Jones, Hoot Gibson, Tim McCoy, Bob Steele, and more.

Coming along so early in the history of film, Tom Mix, a genuine cowboy, helped to establish the visual image of the on-screen cowboy hero. The following description that appeared in *TIME* magazine will serve as a generalization of the western action on screen in the silent film era:

> The Good Guy wore a white hat, the Bad Guy wore a black hat. G.G. was clean-shaven, B.G. had 5 o'clock shadow, and an experienced horse fan could predict the depth of the villain's depravity by checking the length of his sideburns. The villain chased the hero from right to left, but when the hero was winning, he was naturally headed right (with his pistol hand closest to the camera). Anybody shot was assumed dead, unless the audience was notified to the contrary. The stock situations had also been worked out—the stage robbery, the Indian attack, the big stampede, the necktie party, the chair-throwing brawl in the barroom—and in the subtitles, the dialogue had been perfected: "We'll head 'em off at the pass!" ("Westerns: The Six-Gun Galahad", *TIME*, March 30, 1959).

Tom Mix achieved fame as Hollywood's first Western superstar in films made from 1909 through 1935, all but nine of them being silent movies. His earliest films were performed in more of a documentary style, such as seen in his 1910 film, *Ranch Life in the Great Southwest*, in which he demonstrated cattle wrangling skills. His movies made throughout the 1920s would feature action-packed stories in which he would "save the day" as the cowboy hero. Tom was known for doing his own stunts in his films. Adding to his image and fame was his intelligent, good-looking, black horse, Tony, who became a celebrity, as well!

Though Mix died in a car crash in 1940, his fame continued by way of a Fawcett comic book series and a radio show. Such was the height of his popularity that the comic book series was popular through the early years of television, published during the years 1948-1953.

Beginning in 1933, Ralston-Purina produced a radio series, *Tom Mix Ralston Straight Shooters*, featuring an actor portraying the cowboy hero, Tom Mix (Mix himself never appeared on the program). Tom, with his horse Tony, lived on the TM-Bar Ranch with his elderly sidekick and ranch hand, "the Old Wrangler," and cared for young orphans, Jane and Jimmy.

The Ralston Company promoted its cereals with ads to which a youngster could respond and receive special Tom Mix comic books and join the Straight Shooters Club. In their "Tom Mix Ralston Straight Shooters of America Secret Manual" was found the Straight Shooters' Pledge.

The Straight Shooters' Pledge

- As a loyal American and faithful follower of Tom Mix, I pledge allegiance to his Ralston Straight Shooters of America and promise to obey, to the best of my ability, the following rules:
- I promise to shoot straight with my parents by obeying my father and mother, and by eating the food they want me to eat.
- I promise to shoot straight with my friends by telling the truth always, by being fair and square in work or play, by trying always to win, and by being a good loser if I lose.
- I promise to shoot straight with myself, by striving to always be at my best, by keeping my mind alert and my body strong and healthy.
- I promise to shoot straight with Tom Mix by regularly eating Ralston, Official Straight Shooters' Cereal, because I know Ralston is just the kind of cereal that will help build a stronger America.

Buck Jones

In 1937-1938, the short-lived radio program *Hoofbeats* ran in syndication, starring one of the most famous western movie heroes, Charles "Buck" Jones. Sponsored in part by Post Grape Nuts Flakes cereal, the show was a drama that featured a character named the "Old Wrangler" narrating stories about a drifting cowboy – Buck – and his horse, Silver.

Buck Jones was a great horse rider who became a major western star in the silent film era. Fortunately for Jones, his voice recorded well when movies became "talkies" allowing him to continue as a western star in the film industry of the 1930s. His film career was still going strong when he died along with almost 400 other people in the infamous Boston Cocoanut Grove fire on November 28, 1942.

During his successful movie career in the mid-1930s, Buck Jones began appearing in various comic book titles as well as some Big Little Book stories. Like Tom Mix, he died before he could have a chance to star in his own television program, but he still remained popular as a western star during the early years of television. A Dell-published comic book series bearing his name and likeness ran during the early 1950s and sold well enough to continue with a once-a-year issue from 1954 until 1957.

In a June, 1937 broadcast of *Hoofbeats*, the young fans of Buck Jones were given the opportunity to join the Buck Jones Club by mailing in a box top from Grape Nuts Flakes. In return, they could receive a free membership badge and such free prizes as cowboy boots, a hat, western chaps, and a club manual. Buck Jones also had his own creed for his club members. The creed is relatively brief, but includes many of the same values found in the other cowboy codes.

Buck Jones Cowboy Creed

- I must be courteous and obedient to my elders.
- I must study and learn.
- I must be courageous, honest, industrious, truthful and unselfish.
- I must be a pal to my playmates and big brother (or big sister) to all boys or girls younger than myself.
- I must keep my life bright and clean.

Wild Bill Hickok

OPENING CREDITS: On screen, Wild Bill Hickok and Jingles are seen riding their horses as you hear the announcer speak:

ANNOUNCER: Kellogg's, the greatest name in cereal, presents...
JINGLES: Wild Bill Hickok!
ANNOUNCER: Starring Guy Madison as Wild Bill Hickok...
JINGLES: Hey, Wild Bill, wait for me!...
ANNOUNCER: And Andy Devine as his pal, Jingles.
[Wild Bill is then seen aiming and shooting his gun in the direction of the camera as the screen fades to black.]

Wild Bill Hickok was a ratings hit on television that aired in syndication from April 15, 1951 through May 16, 1958. Consisting of 113 half-hour episodes, the show proved to have sustaining popularity and was subsequently seen in reruns on both CBS and ABC. In general, the show was quite similar to the other B westerns of early 1950s television, as aptly described in 1955 in *Broadcasting*: "The pattern for this series has pretty well evolved along basic patterns - there is the hero, his amusing saddle sidekick for comic relief, the villains and a few others who only get in the way, like the sheriff and girl." (*Broadcasting*, June 13, 1955). What gave the show a level of distinction from its competition was the portrayal of an Old West legend, Wild Bill Hickok, and the exceptional performance of Andy Devine in his role as the gravel-voiced sidekick, Jingles P. Jones.

The series was also known for its high production values. It was filmed in black and white, with the exception of seasons five and seven, which were filmed in color. The final 13 episodes were produced in 1958 by new owner Screen Gems and were also filmed in color. The series could boast of the reputation it had gained for excellent photography and well-written and well-acted characterizations. Even the commercial spots for *Wild Bill Hickok* were apparently memorable, as noted in a trade magazine: "Equally sprightly, along with the photography, are the animated commercials for Kellogg's Sugar Smacks, Corn Flakes and Rice Krispies. Krispies includes a special offer of pet statuettes for 'horse- trading' purposes." (*Broadcasting*, June 13, 1955). In 1954, the show was nominated for an Emmy as "Best Western or Adventure Series."

For most of the period of 1951-1956, a *Wild Bill Hickok* radio series broadcast on the Mutual network ran concurrently with the television series. The radio version of the show was sponsored by Kellogg Cereals and also starred Guy Madison and Andy Devine in the same roles they played on television. The radio show proved to be quite popular with listeners. In 1953, *Wild Bill Hickok* was the number three program in the ratings for the weekday listening audiences, trailing only two Arthur Godfrey programs.

Strongly identified with the B western heroes of 1950s television – along with the hero's horse – was the ever-present sidekick. At least one entire book (*Those Great Cowboy Sidekicks* by David Rothel) has been written to pay tribute to the iconic role. Among the many to have played the part of the hero's pal, Andy Devine has been considered by more than a few critics to have been the best of the group with his portrayal of Wild Bill's comic sidekick, Jingles. Western author Raymond White wrote that when it came to "portraying a befuddled yet humorous and charismatic partner to a western hero," it is likely that no one did it better than Andy Devine. He was a key part of the success of *Wild Bill Hickok*.

The Wild Bill Hickok Deputy Marshal's Code of Conduct

1. I will be brave, but never careless.
2. I will obey my parents. They DO know best.
3. I will be neat and clean at all times.
4. I will be polite and courteous.
5. I will protect the weak and help them.
6. I will study hard.
7. I will be kind to animals and care for them.
8. I will respect my flag and my country.
9. I will attend my place of worship regularly.

Tales of the Texas Rangers

OPENING CREDITS: Each episode of *Tales of the Texas Rangers* opened with a close-up shot of Jace Pearson, then the camera angle widened as additional uniformed Texas Rangers joined him in the middle of the street while the opening theme song played: "Here's a stalwart man of Texas / Jace Pearson is his name / His partner Clay is right beside him / Each day adds to their fame / All Texas Rangers sworn to duty / Their work is never through / They fight and fight for rights and justice / to enforce the law for you."

Tales of the Texas Rangers first appeared as a radio series in July, 1950, on the NBC radio network, lasting until September, 1952. The show was formatted in a style similar to radio's *Dragnet* and stories were set in modern times and based on actual Texas Ranger case histories. It then came to television as a 30-minute black-and-white series, airing from August 27, 1955 through December 26, 1958 on CBS. Unlike the radio series, the stories in the television series were not based on actual cases.

The series, which starred Willard Parker as Ranger Jace Pearson and Harry Lauter as his partner Clay Morgan, represented a new twist on the television western. The weekly stories alternated between the historical 1800s time period and the present day adventures of the Texas Rangers. Each episode was introduced by Jace who was seen reading from either "Volume 1: The Early Days" or "Volume 2: Today" of the Texas Rangers scrapbooks. In one of the early episodes, the two Rangers explained to the audience that the "Early Days" stories were tales of the exploits of their grandfathers – who coincidentally had identical names and looks to themselves. Thus, the same two actors starred in each story, whether the setting was historical or modern.

Like many other series that targeted a juvenile audience, *Tales of the Texas Rangers* was sponsored by a breakfast cereal company – in this case, Corn Kix cereal – and an alternate sponsor, the Curtiss Candy Company. An example of a typical sponsor spot identifying the sponsor for a given week would be similar to this Curtiss Candy message appearing at the end of the opening theme: "*Tales of the Texas Rangers* - brought to you by Curtiss Candy Company, makers of delicious Baby Ruth candy bars and crispy, crunchy Butterfinger candy bars!"

In 1956, Curtiss Candy Company also ran a commercial tie-in promotion for the show with a premium offer to kids in the viewing audience. Any young fan of the show could become a Tales of the Texas Rangers Deputy by mailing to company headquarters two wrappers from Curtiss candy bars – either Baby Ruth or Butterfinger – and 25 cents. The promo spokesman, appearing in a Tales of the Texas Rangers uniform, promised that in return, each new 'deputy' would then receive an "official deputy star in bright, silvery metal with real raised letters, and this terrific, silvery deputy ring, a special deputy identification card like this with your own official number, the Ranger Oath, space for your name and address, and – best of all – a place for your signature alongside Jace Pearson's. Isn't that great!" The Ranger Oath contained similar values to those already seen in one or more cowboy hero codes, as seen below.

Texas Rangers "Deputy Ranger" Oath

1. Be Alert
2. Be Obedient
3. Defend the Weak
4. Never Desert a Friend
5. Never Take Unfair Advantage
6. Be Neat
7. Be Truthful
8. Uphold Justice
9. Live Cleanly
10. Have Faith in God

Bobby Benson's B-Bar-B Riders

OPENING CREDITS (radio version): "Here they come! They're riding fast and they're riding hard! It's time for excitement and adventure in the modern West with Bobby Benson and his B-Bar-B Riders! And out in front, astride his golden palomino Amigo, it's the Cowboy Kid." (This is an example of the high-energy narration used to introduce an episode of the highly popular radio program in the early 1950s.)

Two television series featuring the popular radio cowboy were produced by WOR-TV, based on the popular radio series, "Bobby Benson's B-Bar-B Riders." The television show never reached the fame of the radio program, which actually had two incarnations. The first *Bobby Benson* radio series ran on network radio in 1932-1936 and was one of the first juvenile audience-oriented shows on radio. The second version of the series, under the title "Bobby Benson's B-Bar-B Riders," ran on the Mutual radio network from 1949-1955.

The radio series starred five regular characters: Bobby, Tex, Windy, Harka, and Irish. They lived and worked together on the B-Bar-B Ranch, with Tex Mason as the foreman. The old geezer, Windy Wales, was played by Don Knotts, then in his mid-20s. (He is the same actor who would later create the iconic Deputy Barney Fife on television's *The Andy Griffith Show*.) Bobby's horse on the radio show was a golden palomino named Amigo. By 1950, the 30-minute show was airing nationally at least five days each week.

The move to television was accomplished by a local station in the New York market, WOR-TV. The first of two television versions starred the radio cast and was shot live at the New Amsterdam Theater before moving to a studio on West 66th Street. It was a 30-minute show sponsored by Foxe's "U-Bet" Chocolate Syrup. In one of the promotion campaigns for the show, a live pony was given away to contest winners. The second TV version of *Bobby Benson* was shot in the mid-1950s at the same Channel 9 studios, on a set that consisted of a tiny bunkhouse, employing a small cast. It was sponsored by Wilrich's Grape Drink.

However, the lasting legacy of *Bobby Benson* is the radio show that lasted until mid-1955, totaling over 350 episodes, and a vast, national listening audience. The actor(s) portraying Bobby Benson made public appearances throughout the United States, visiting children's hospitals, orphanages, appearing in parades, and more. The character and the show were quite popular, and Bobby Benson merchandise sold in large quantities in stores alongside that of Hoppy, Gene, Roy, the Lone Ranger, the Cisco Kid, and Red Ryder. In 1950, a series of comic books was published that ran for 20 issues, ending in 1953.

In the "Model Fun" comic book series, each issue contained stories and lots of 'how to' information for crafts and hobbies such as model air planes and boats. Included on the back cover of the "Model Fun" issue No. 4, published in May, 1955, was the following Bobby Benson Rider's Pledge:

I Pledge Myself . . .
- To Trust in God.
- To be loyal to my Country and my Flag.
- To be a good Citizen.
- To make Safety my Watchword.
- To help Others with their Hobbies.

Cowboy G-Men

The B western TV series heroes considered to this point have all had their own written, published code of the west. As we have seen, most of them were presented as a ten-point listing of rules by which to live and behave. However, there were some cowboy heroes among early TV's B westerns who, while they had no written or published creed, nonetheless adhered to the same values and ideals expressed in the written codes. *Cowboy G-Men* is an example of this.

Starring Russell Hayden as Pat Gallagher and Jackie Coogan as Stoney Crockett, *Cowboy G-Men* was an action-packed, B western with many of the usual western film trappings. However, it was distinct in that the main characters were actually government agents working as secret service men in the Old West, and typically shown working undercover on some dangerous special assignment. The short-lived series originally ran in syndication from September, 1952 through June, 1953.

The author is unaware of any published creed or code associated with *Cowboy G-Men*. However, the value of having such a set of rules was evident in a campaign by the show's sponsor. Taystee Bread, in an ad campaign for the series, invited youngsters to set up a list of rules to live by in their print ads for Taystee Bread. The ad read as follows:

Start your own G-MEN CLUB! It's easy! Hold regular meetings – elect officers – have a password like 'That's for Sure!' Set up a list of rules to always do what is right just as Pat and Stoney do – and keep watching them on TV! (Advertisement, undated).

Local Market Cowboys

"Every TV station has some sort [of] Western film program, many going by names like *Six-Gun Playhouse* or *Frontier Theatre*," noted *Sponsor* magazine in an article in their September 25, 1950 issue. The article continued:

Youngsters, however, are the primary target of Western programing on TV. The situation in New York City is typical: Out of some 53 Western film programs shown on seven stations in a recent week, no less than 46 were scheduled to end before 8:00 p.m. ... Some 23 out of the 53 are aimed unmistakably at kids. They have live beginnings with small-fry audiences, kid-club doings, and commercials keyed to juvenile thinking. The commercials plug such products as children's shoes, breakfast cereal, milk, bread, ice cream, toys, chewing gum, and candy. (*Sponsor*, September 25, 1950).

By the early 1950s, television stations had discovered that locally-produced, kid-oriented shows – such as those described in the preceding paragraph – were very popular with their viewing audience. The shows usually were staffed by local station talent, including the cast, filling the allotted air time with whatever entertainment they could manage to pull off. More often than not, these shows relied upon incorporating the extensive use of westerns and cartoons. The shows also benefitted from the excitement of having a live studio audience consisting of children from the local viewing area. Having local children on camera had a measurable economic benefit – it helped sell TV sets! In the early 1950s, TV sets were expensive; however, parents did not want to miss seeing their children on screen whenever they appeared on their favorite local show.

Many stations across the nation hosted their own kid-oriented live show, usually with a western flavor. In New York, for example, there was a 15-minute kids' western, *Mystery Rider*, as well as a daily one-hour show called *Western Roundup*, with Ranger Lyle Reed hosting, and sponsored locally by Fischer Baking Company. In Columbus, Ohio, youngsters could tune in daily from 4:30 to 6:00 to watch their own *Western Roundup*. They would then be entertained by The Wrangler and Blackie who fascinated the kids with their western lore, cowboy rope tricks and stories highlighted with the drawing of exclusive personal brands for youngsters who had completed "achievement" cards.

We will now look a bit more closely at three such local shows, and their connection with the cowboy Code of the West theme of this book: *The Old Rebel and Pecos Pete Show* in Greensboro, North Carolina; *Pick Temple* in the Washington, D.C. area, and the *Ghost Riders* in Philadelphia.

Greensboro's *The Old Rebel and Pecos Pete Show*

Airing weekdays at 5:00 p.m. on WFMY-TV, *The Old Rebel and Pecos Pete Show* was a ratings winner for the station in the Greensboro, North Carolina market. The show starred George Perry as the Old Rebel, always wearing a black top hat, frock coat, and an old-fashioned bow tie. His sidekick, Pecos Pete, was played by Jim Tucker, who displayed a wide range of western talents, including rope tricks, sharp-shooting, and guitar playing. The show began in the early 1950s and enjoyed a very long run, lasting until the mid-1960s.

The show capitalized on the popularity of the western genre, and at times included interviews with big stars like Gene Autry and Dennis Weaver. However, as the stars of a local show, the Old Rebel and Pecos Pete were much more accessible heroes to the local youngsters. Over the years, the two made countless appearances in the area, further endearing themselves to their audience in the process.

As with most, if not all, local shows of this type, a critical element of the show's format was the presence of local children in the studio, on set and on camera, as a part of each day's show. A fan club was also established that allowed the children an additional way to connect with the show. By 1964, the Old Rebel and Pecos Pete Club boasted 15,000 members!

With a membership in the Old Rebel and Pecos Pete Club, came a membership card, and a flyer that contained a copy of the club's song, the club's creed, and the "Five Simple Rules" to live by.

Five Simple Rules:
1. I will try to be honest at all times.
2. I will try to be helpful to my family and others.
3. I will try to be kind to my playmates and to animals.
4. I will try to work harder in school to learn all I can.
5. I will practice safety rules at home, in school, and on the street.

The Old Rebel and Pecos Pete Club's creed (as it appeared on the outside of the envelope in which the membership kit for the Old Rebel and Pecos Pete Club was mailed):

"I, [club members name], will try to live by the rules of the Old Rebel and Pecos Pete Club to the best of my ability, and obey my parents and teachers."

Washington D.C.'s *The Pick Temple Giant Ranch*

From 1950 to 1961, the Giant Food grocery store chain and Heidi Bread sponsored *The Pick Temple Giant Ranch*, a show that aired live daily in the Washington, D.C. television market. The show featured in-studio participation from its audience consisting of children from the viewing area. The show was extremely popular, with an estimated 250,000 children from ages 3 to 16 having joined Pick Temple's Giant Ranger club during the decade the show was on the air.

The star and host of the show was Pick Temple, along with his collie, "Lady," and "Piccolo," the pony. Broadcast live daily from local studios, the show included audience participation, as well as the viewing of old Western films (featuring cowboy stars like Tim McCoy, Kit Carson, and Bill Williams), games, puppets, songs (Pick sang and played guitar), and cartoons – and of course, lots of commercial plugs for Giant grocery stores. On screen, noted Pick's son, Parker Temple, Pick "never talked down to the kids, never played the buffoon. He was…the inveterate teacher."

As noted previously, local cowboys were more accessible to their audiences, and Pick and Giant both received the benefits resulting from the countless appearances Pick made throughout the area over the years. Pick became a trusted friend for the youngsters who faithfully tuned in to the show and met him in public. Parents must also have appreciated Pick's style. One viewer recalled that "if it were a nice day, Pick might turn to the camera and say, 'You kids ought to consider going out to play instead of watching TV.'"

Like other respectable cowboy heroes, Pick had a club which youngsters could join, along with applicable membership items and a club pledge regarding rules of conduct. To become a Pick Temple Giant Ranger Cowhand, a youngster simply obtained and mailed a pre-addressed business reply card from one of the Giant grocery stores in the area. From this, the child received a cowhand button, a membership card and Ranger pledge, a health chart, and a letter of welcome.

The enclosed health chart was an important step in encouraging proper behavior from the young club members. On it, the child was to note his accomplishments during each month on the health chart. It would then be countersigned by his mother (the "bunkhouse foreman") and returned to Giant Ranch headquarters. The youngster would then receive a ranch hand button and a Range Rule chart outlining simplified "rules of living."

Completing that second chart would lead to even more material from Giant Ranch headquarters.

The Pledge of a Pick Temple's Giant Ranger:
"I will live up to the creed of a Pick Temple Ranger to carry on the principles of Good Citizenship to help the needy, aged and sick, to respect my parents and teachers, to love my neighbors, city and country. Don't put off until tomorrow what you can do today."

Philadelphia's *Ghost Riders*

By 1950, in the Philadelphia television market, *Ghost Riders* was on the air at 5:30 every weekday evening. The episodes typically featured a full-length western film plus updates on the activities of The Ghost Rider's Club members – which had already attracted 24,000 members just seven months after it was started! When a new member joined the club, they received 10 "performance cards" that their mother could mail in to the station listing the child's good deeds, as well as any other comments on their behavior. These cards were then entered into a drawing from which winners could obtain prizes that included Gene Autry and Roy Rogers merchandise items.

The Ghost Rider's Club, as may be expected had their own pledge, as seen below. Note that the pledge could be presented in the form of an acrostic.

The Ghost Rider pledge:
A true Ghost Rider does one good turn for Mother each day.
He does his homework early.
Orderly and tidy habits mark his path.
Studying is important to a real Ghost Rider.
Thoughtfulness of others is part of his code.
Riders brush their teeth every day.
Industrious and active minds make an alert Rider.
Doing little chores that Mother asks.
Every Rider cleans his dinner plate at mealtime.
Remember to watch for the Ghost Rider every day at 5:30 p.m., on Channel 10.

This full-page ad appeared in Fawcett's May, 1948 issue of *Tom Mix Western* comics.

In the screenshots inset in the image above, a spokesman, appearing in a *Tales of the Texas Rangers* uniform, promised that each new "Tales of the Texas Ranger Deputy" would receive an "official deputy star in bright, silvery metal with real raised letters, and … a special deputy identification card like this with your own official number, the Ranger Oath, space for your name and address, …"

HELLO THERE!

B-B RIDERS AND MODEL BUILDERS

Here is some very exciting news I have for you! You can become a member of the Bobby Benson Hobby Clubs and get a membership card—all your own—just like the one shown here!

It's very easy to become a member . . . all you do is go to your local hobby shop where you can get **your** membership card free.

There are ten Hobby Clubs to choose from; as you will see . . . and your membership card tells you also how you can obtain many exciting Bobby Benson projects and plans!

So, B-B Riders, join me in my hobbies by becoming a member and get your official membership card today!

I'll be giving you more news about the Bobby Benson Clubs on my show, over your local Mutual Station each week-day, when you'll hear me and all my friends at the B-B too . . . Windy Wales and Tex Mason; Cactus Carl; Not forgetting Amigo, my trusted Palomino; and Hero, my dog and best freind!

Adios Amigos!

Your friend, *Bobby Benson*

MEMBERSHIP CARD
BOBBY BENSON CREATIVE CRAFT

(Name of your club)

HOBBY CLUB.

(Rider's Name)

Bobby Benson

BOBBY

Signed-"The Hobby Boy of America."

EXPIRES DECEMBER 31st, 1955

THE BOBBY BENSON RIDER'S PLEDGE

I Pledge Myself . . . .
- To Trust in God.
- To be loyal to my Country and my Flag.
- To be a good Citizen.
- To make Safety my Watchword.
- To help Others with their Hobbies.

BOBBY BENSON CREATIVE CRAFT HOBBY CLUBS
a. Arts & Crafts   f. Needlecraft Sewing & Weaving
b. Camping, Biking & Hiking   g. Pets
c. Collecting Hobbies   h. Photography
d. Drama, Music & Literature   j. Writing—"pen pals."
e. Model Building   i. Sports

DEALERS STAMP
Dealer—Please stamp your name and address to validate card.

Dealers: To obtain your Bobby Benson Creative Craft Hobby Club membership cards free, contact your local Mutual Station, or obtain them direct from Bobby Benson, c/o Richard S. Robbins Co., 163 Bleecker St., New York 12, N. Y.

The Bobby Benson Rider's Pledge appeared on the back cover of the May, 1955, issue of *Model Fun* comics.

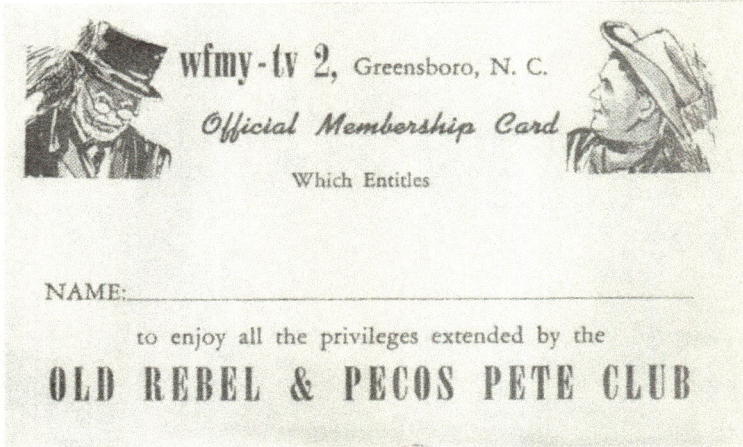

Materials for members of The Old Rebel & Pecos Pete Club included a membership card (shown above) and a copy of the Old Rebel's "Five Simple Rules."

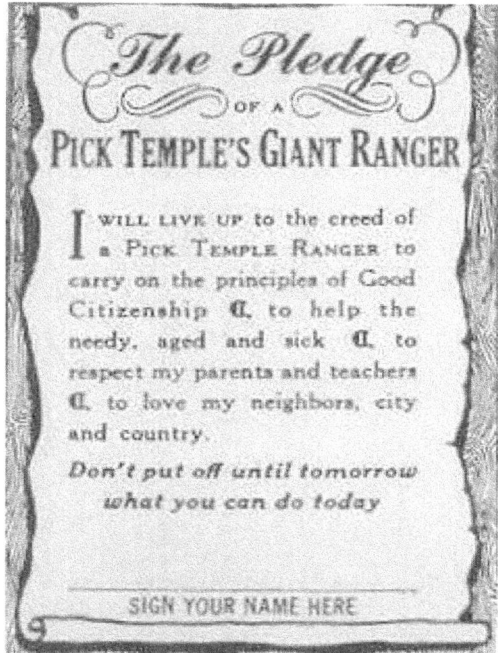

(*Below*) Advertisement promoting the *Pick Temple's Giant Ranch* show.

(*Above*) Each Pick Temple Ranger received their own copy of The Pledge of a Pick Temple Giant Ranger.

7

ROLE MODELS WITH UNWRITTEN CODES

The focus of this book is upon the B western television cowboy heroes who had a written and published creed or code. However, many other B western heroes appeared on 1950s television screens who, while they did not have their own published code of rules to live by, were nonetheless prime examples of heroes adhering to the same ideals and values embraced by their fellow cowboy heroes. In a sense, they were following the un-written code of the west, and most took seriously the fact they were serving as role models to their young viewers. In this chapter, we will briefly discuss some of these early TV cowboy heroes who, without a written code of their own, were in their own way adhering to the same values and principles expressed in the written codes, as evidenced by their episodic story content and the industry-related media and publicity at the time.

Flying A Productions

We will begin with the various shows produced by Gene Autry's Flying A Productions. As already seen, Gene Autry was successful in his foray into television with his own *Gene Autry Show*, and that success led to the production of additional "Flying A" heroes: *The Range Rider* (1951-53), *Annie Oakley* (1954-57), *Buffalo Bill, Jr.*(1955-56), and *The Adventures of Champion* (1955-56).

These shows were put together with the same production values and care that characterized Gene's show. For example, when *The Range Rider* first became available for television broadcasts, potential sponsors were courted with the advance notice that the same advertising limitations in place for Gene's show would also apply to other Flying A productions. "As in the case of *Gene Autry* sponsorship, beer, cigarette, wine and deodorant advertising is not accepted," noted an ad to attract potential sponsors for *The Range Rider* in a 1951 issue of the trade magazine, *Sponsor*. The same general sales pitch was again used when *Buffalo Bill, Jr.* was later developed for television. An ad in a 1955 issue of *Sponsor* soliciting advertisers for the new show noted it was "produced to the same standards which have made *Gene Autry*, *The Range Rider* and *Annie Oakley* the hottest Westerns in television year after year."

The Range Rider

OPENING CREDITS:

> BACKGROUND SINGERS: *"Home, home on the range, where the deer and the antelope play"*
>
> ANNOUNCER: And who could be more at home on the range than the Range Rider! - with his thrilling adventures of the great outdoors; his exciting experiences rivaling those of Davy Crockett, Daniel Boone, Buffalo Bill, and other pioneers of this wonderful country of ours .... and Dick West, All-American Boy.

The star of the show was Jack ("Jock") Mahoney, who prior to starring in *Range Rider* was primarily a stunt rider. As a relatively unknown name when the show began and playing a new character, the Range Rider, the network felt the need to provide additional promotion of *The Range Rider* to help it compete with the other cowboy stars already on the air at the time (Autry, Rogers, Hopalong, the Cisco Kid, and the Lone Ranger). In early 1952, the network sponsored a 20-day, cross-country personal appearance tour for Mahoney. During the tour, he drew large crowds by showing up at department stores, super-markets, recreation parks, parades, hospitals, schools, orphanages, and radio and TV show interview programs.

The show quickly attracted an audience and, like the other B western heroes, Mahoney was in demand for personal appearances, including frequent visits to children in hospitals. A typical report was like this one, following a 1952 visit to Rochester, New York: "His two television appearances, as guest on Ross Weller's afternoon show and Bob Turner's evening show, permitted many more Mahoney fans to see their hero – which is just what he is to them – a hero. Whether you like a cowboy or not, you can't help but like Mahoney as a person." (*TV Life*, April 26-May 2, 1952).

Annie Oakley

OPENING CREDITS (syndicated version): "Bulls-eye! ... Annie Oakley hits the entertainment bull's-eye each week with her hard riding ... straight shooting ... and suspense."

Television's *Annie Oakley* starred Gail Davis in the title role. She had previously appeared in many movies and television episodes for Gene Autry, who called her "a perfect Western heroine." Co-starring in the role of Tagg Oakley was Jimmy Hawkins, who could rope, ride and shoot, and he could handle horses as a boy. Set in the fictional town of Diablo, Arizona, Annie lived with her kid brother, Tagg, and throughout the series was frequently seen assisting Deputy Sheriff Lofty Craig.

The show's version of Annie Oakley bore little resemblance to the historical Annie Oakley. For example, the historical figure won her fame with the use of a rifle, while the fictional version played by Gail Davis used

"For years, Autry had wanted to produce a series of motion pictures which would establish the first girl Western star. As Gene says, 'Little boys have had their idols—Tom Mix, William S. Hart, Buck Jones and, later, Roy Rogers and me — from the beginning of the picture business. They've always had it over their sisters in this respect, because little girls had to idolize the same stars—all men. Why not give the girls a female Western star of their own?'"

("Golden Girl (Annie Oakley)," *Radio TV Mirror*, January, 1957.)

two pistols almost exclusively. The television personification of Annie was aptly described by *TV Guide* in a 1954 article: "Since Annie is a female-type gal, she doesn't get into any knockdown, drag-out affairs with the villains. But the way she handles those six-shooters, she doesn't have to use her fists."

As portrayed and embodied by Gail Davis, the Annie Oakley character caught on with audiences who appreciated that she exhibited a feminine nurturing characteristic along with the more masculine qualities of spunk and toughness. To some degree, Gail's appearance seemed to be modeled after that of Dale Evans, with her western boots, bandana, fringed vest, and split skirt — and wearing of pistols — yielding a visual image not that different from Evans'. However, the character of Annie generally outrode and outshot all of her male character counterparts, making the show distinct from the other B westerns of the 1950s.

Buffalo Bill, Jr.

OPENING CREDITS: As the viewer watches Buffalo Bill, Jr. perform some trick-riding and action sequences:

> SINGERS: *"Buffalo Bill, Jr.! ..."*
> ANNOUNCER: Buffalo Bill, Jr.! With his little sister, Calamity! *Buffalo Bill, Jr.* brings you exciting action! Thrills! And fun! With Judge Ben Fair-and-Square Wiley!
> SINGERS: *"Buffalo Bill - Buffalo Bill – Buffalo Bill – Buffalo Bill - Junior!"*

Dick Jones had co-starred in *The Range Rider*, and was sufficiently talented and popular to be given the chance by Gene Autry to star in his own show. *Buffalo Bill, Jr.* was set in a pioneer town with Buffalo Bill, Jr. and his kid sister, Calamity, as two young orphans that had been adopted by the town's elderly judge. The series' episodes followed their adventures and frequently showcased the horsemanship of Dick Jones.

By the time he was five years of age, Dick was an accomplished trick rider and roper in rodeos. By the time he was appearing in *Buffalo Bill, Jr.*, *TV Guide* noted, "It's nothing for him to leap from his galloping mount atop an outlaw riding at top speed, knock him to the ground and best him in a slugfest." He was simply a natural horseman and stunt rider from boyhood, having worked as a young boy off camera with Hoot Gibson, and

> "Sunday morning at ten o'clock, you'll find Dick Jones — personable young Buffalo Bill, Jr., of the two-to-teen set—suited out in his best go-to-meetin' clothes, perched squarely in the middle of the front pew of Hollywood's First Presbyterian Church. With the shy smile that has thrown a lariat around several million hero-hungry hearts, Dick says in his easy Texas drawl, 'I sit down front so's I can stretch my legs way out and see what's going on better.'"
>
> ("Keeping Up With The Joneses", by Gordon Budge, *Radio TV Mirror*, Atlantic Edition, September, 1957)

with eleven Buck Jones movies on his resume prior to working for Flying A Productions. Dick was reportedly the perfect actor for the role of Buffalo Bill, Jr., with a reputation for being a young man of great integrity and high moral character.

Dick Jones and his wife were active in the Hollywood Christian Group in the 1950s, and were outspoken about their Christian faith. He and his wife had four children at the time, and took seriously their responsibility as parents for the spiritual upbringing of their children. Dick's wife, Betty, told of how they helped their children to learn Bible verses, and taught their children how to pray on their own. She said, "We simply want them to learn that they can go to God, that He is with them all the time . . ." and that, as parents, "our one goal in life is the hope that we'll be able to teach them each day to live as He would want them to." ("Keeping Up With The Joneses", *Radio TV Mirror*, September, 1957).

The Adventures of Champion

OPENING CREDITS: "Champion the Wonder Horse! Champion the Wonder Horse! / Like a streak of lightnin' flashin' cross the sky, / Like the swiftest arrow whistlin' from a bow, / Like a mighty cannonball he seems to fly. / You'll hear about him ever'where you go. / The time'll come when everyone will know / The name of Champion the Wonder Horse!"

Set on a ranch in the American Southwest, *The Adventures of Champion* aired on CBS during the 1955-56 season and starred young Barry Curtis as 12-year-old Ricky North, and Jim Bannon as Ricky's Uncle Sandy North – and, of course, featured "Champion, the Wonder Horse." In the series' premise, young Ricky was befriended by Champion, a wild stallion, and was accompanied by his German Shepherd, Rebel.

Gene Autry's horse, Champion, was the star of the show, and was already famous from *The Gene Autry Show*, and some 85 Autry films, as well as Autry's personal appearances in rodeos and other promotional tours. Evidence of the appeal of Champion to a young audience was provided by the Champion-titled comic books which were selling at a pace of about three million copies annually in the mid-1950s.

The show was promoted by CBS as another fine program that embraced the production values of Flying A Productions. After its one-season run, an ad promoting the show for syndication appeared in *Television Magazine*, quoting Billboard's evaluation of the show that emphasized its suitability for children: "*Champion* is solid entertainment, excellent production...over all, the kind of fare that parents can sit down with their children to watch!" (*Television Magazine*, May 1956).

Sky King – "America's Flying Cowboy"

OPENING CREDITS (syndicated version): "From out of the blue of the western sky comes Sky King!" As those words are spoken, the viewer sees Sky's plane, the Songbird, flying through the sky.

Sky King first began as a radio adventure program in October, 1946, before beginning on NBC television in 1951. The TV show then moved to ABC in 1952, before going into syndication from 1955-1959. The star of the TV version was "Sky" King, a former Navy flyer, played by Kirby Grant. Both the radio and television versions of the show were sponsored by Peter Pan Peanut Butter.

In the television series, *Sky King* was the story of Arizona rancher and airplane pilot, Schuyler "Sky" King, and his adventures near the fictional town of Grover, Arizona. Joining him were his teenaged niece, Penny, and nephew, Clipper. Both of them were also pilots, though relatively inexperienced, and lived with Sky on his "Flying Crown Ranch." The series was a western, often involving action with horses and guns, but in each episode, Sky chiefly relied upon the use of his plane, a Cessna T-50 twin-engine plane called the "Songbird" to help capture villains and rescue lost or endangered hikers, hunters, and so on.

Many pilots later attributed the inspiration for their careers in aviation to *Sky King*. Kirby Grant was well aware that to many youngsters across the nation in the 1950s, he was a role model and a hero. In his recollections about the series, the reader will note some similarity between his comments and the elements of the Code of the West discussed earlier in this book. Kirby Grant recalled that:

> We portrayed a family unit even though it was an uncle, niece and nephew. Anything I can do to instill the idea of settling disputes peacefully in the minds of my young audience is of paramount importance. I tried to remain responsive to my image. I did enjoy a drink, but I never took one near kids. I never smoked near them and I watched my language. It all had the tendency to make a better person of me. I tried to live up to the character I portrayed. I think kids need a knight in shining armor. They'll grow up and find things different, but it doesn't hurt to have heroes while they're young. Role models aren't there anymore. If I never do anything else in my life, at least I know I've accomplished something good. I've had young people in their 30's come up to me and say, 'I'm in military flying or I'm a commercial pilot or somehow engaged in the aircraft industry, only because I watched your show.' That makes me feel good, to think I've done something very constructive. (retrieved December 29, 2014 from WesternClippings.com).

The Adventures of Kit Carson

Starring Bill Williams as "Kit" Carson, *The Adventures of Kit Carson* originally aired in syndication from 1951-1955, and was sponsored by Coca-Cola. Don Diamond co-starred as Kit's Mexican sidekick, "El Toro." Together, Kit Carson and El Toro wandered throughout the West always ready to help those in need.

The show, though it was only a fictionalized account of Kit's life, earned a good reputation with parents and teachers. The impact of the show – and the desire of its star to be a positive influence on the youth of the day – was highlighted in a 1955 *TV Radio Mirror* article:

> Because of a minimum of violence and a devotion to historical fact, the program has been recommended by church groups and the PTA. Bill is pleased with this support. Ever since he was a kid living in the hard heart of Brooklyn, he's wanted to combat delinquency and juvenile problems. As plain 'Bill Williams,' he's just another voice. But, as TV's clean-living Kit Carson, he's the voice of an army of 10,000,000. On television, he can reach more kids in a week than he could in a year—and they are influenced by what he has to say. As an example of Bill's influence with youngsters, take a recent junior high school contest. The local board of education wanted to name a new school. The winner — the name the children mentioned most frequently — Kit Carson. (*TV Radio Mirror*, January, 1955).

In "real life," Bill Williams and his wife, Barbara, were mindful of the public image they represented. Barbara, who would become known for her role as Perry Mason's sidekick, told reporters she had always been a "working mother" even before starring with Perry Mason. She was active in the PTA, church and charity work, the Camp Fire Girls, and more, but always had maintained a premium on the proper care of their family. Barbara emphasized the shared goals of husband and wife for their family in a 1957 interview: "Point is, that the husband and wife are sharing some common goal, some dream of the future. That's why I don't differentiate between 'working mothers' who may choose to stay at home with their kids, cooking, and PTA — and 'working mothers' who are off to a nine-to-five job. Both are surely working toward some family dream."

The Cisco Kid

OPENING CREDITS: "Here's adventure . . . Here's romance . . . Here's O. Henry's famous Robin Hood of the Old West . . . The Cisco Kid!"

One of the first filmed-for-television shows, production of *The Cisco Kid* began in 1949 by ZIV Productions and the show premiered on the air on September 5, 1950. It was an immediate success and continued to air original episodes through 1956, usually sponsored by a bread company. The show starred Duncan Renaldo in the title role of the Cisco Kid, and Leo

Carrillo as his sidekick, Pancho. The two companions wandered the old Southwest – since they were technically outlaws wanted for some unmentioned crime(s) – fighting injustice and helping others when law enforcement officials were either unavailable, unable, or too corrupt to be any help. The kids viewing the show from home were also familiar with their horses: Cisco's "Diablo," a black and white pinto, and Pancho's "Loco." Like some other B westerns on early TV, the show minimized gunplay, as Duncan Renaldo recalled in a 1970 interview for *TV Guide*: "The Cisco Kid never killed anybody on the show – he found other ways to solve problems."

The Cisco Kid has the distinction of being the first television series to have been filmed in color. Apparently, the folks at ZIV Productions were forward-looking and wanted their show to have the necessary visual appeal to receive airplay once color television came into being. Thus, all 156 episodes were filmed in color, even though extremely few people would see it in color at the time. In 1956, only a miniscule percentage (estimated at 0.05%) of households with a television set had a color set. Even in the mid-1960s, when the major networks began to film and broadcast all their shows in color, only 9.7% of households with a television set had a color set! However, *The Cisco Kid* was still being shown in reruns in the 1970s, so the strategy appears to have paid off.

The show was also distinctive in that its stars were the first regular Hispanic television stars in a series. Renaldo was a native of Romania (and/or Spain) who emigrated to the United States in the early 1920s. Carrillo was a native of Los Angeles, and was already 70 years of age when production of the show began! The Cisco Kid wore an all-black outfit with fancy embroidery, and was a fun-loving, charming, and dashing character. Pancho was also fun-loving, funny, and spoke broken English, becoming known for his catch-phrase, "Ohhh, Ceesco!", whenever he was amused by something that Cisco had done or said.

Duncan Renaldo took seriously his status as a role model for young viewers. Following production of the series, he remained connected with the character in parades, charity drives, and other public appearances. It was reported in *TV Guide* that during his personal appearances, Duncan preferred to downplay the use of guns in the stories he told children. Rather than celebrating the gunmen of the Old West, he chose to tell true stories that pointed up the danger of greed or breaking the law.

Sergeant Preston of the Yukon

OPENING CREDITS: "Sergeant Preston of the Northwest Mounted Police, ...with Yukon King, swiftest and strongest lead dog, ...breaking the trail in the relentless pursuit of lawbreakers in the wild days of the Yukon!"

A snow-covered variation on the B western for television, *Sergeant Preston of the Yukon* was broadcast on CBS from 1955 to 1958, with all 78 episodes filmed in color. The television series was sponsored by Quaker Puffed Wheat and Quaker Puffed Rice, and starred Richard Simmons as Canadian Mountie Sergeant Preston. Also featured in every episode was his faithful lead dog, "Yukon King," usually simply called "King" by Preston, and his horse – for the episodes set in summer – was the black Arabian, "Rex."

The show's premise was similar to the other B westerns of the day, with the hero – Sgt. Preston – apprehending the bad guys while only using his gun to shoot the outlaw's weapons from their hands. Sgt. Preston patrolled in the Yukon Territory during the days of the big Klondike gold rush in the late 1890s. He was kept busy pursuing fur thieves, murderers, claim-jumpers, counterfeiters, smugglers, and other outlaw types. Though Sgt. Preston never used the phrase "always get their man" in the series, in every episode he nonetheless "always got his man." His "wonder dog" King usually played a key role in the capture of the bad guys. At the end of each episode, Sgt. Preston would hug or pat King and say, "Well, King, this case is closed."

Sergeant Preston of the Yukon was the television version of the radio program, "Challenge of the Yukon," which had already been on radio for more than ten years before the television show began. The radio version originated from the WXYZ Detroit radio studios in 1938, and was created by George Trendle, who had already successfully produced *The Lone Ranger* and *Green Hornet* series. Later in life, Trendle talked about the distinct emphasis intended with each of his three signature shows.

'*The Lone Ranger* was produced for kids,' Trendle later recalled. 'The point was to teach the youngsters respect for the law. It was sensible enough to be popular with oldsters as well. Then I put on *Preston* for the teenagers to teach them love for country and love for animals. The third one, *The Green Hornet*, was to appeal to a little older group. The young people about to become voters. I wanted to show them that racketeers and crooked politicians could succeed unless they were stopped.' (as quoted in *The Green Hornet: A History of Radio, Motion Pictures, Comics, and Television*, by Martin Grams, Jr., and Terry Salomonson).

Brave Eagle

This B western television series featuring an American Indian as the lead character – the first TV show to do so – aired on CBS from September, 1955 through March, 1956. The series was produced by Roy Rogers' Frontier Productions and starred Keith Larsen in the title role as Brave Eagle.

The storylines in the episodes of *Brave Eagle* were told from the perspective of the American Indian, with Brave Eagle as the hero and narrator. Plots usually featured stories involving: clashes with warlike tribes, problems with renegade Indians, attempts to prevent war, keeping the tribe's homeland free from encroachment by white settlers, responding to racial and ethnic bias, and the threat of diseases. As the hero of the show, Brave Eagle noted in an early episode, "I stood guard, ready to protect the innocent and the weak."

The episodes also presented a look into the daily lives and activities of the Cheyenne. A 1956 *TV Guide* review of the show pointed out that while the series was "in no sense a documentary, *Brave Eagle* stresses authenticity in scripts and costumes." Adding to the show's authenticity was the cast, which included some actors with American Indian heritage. Keith Larson, as Brave Eagle, was part Cheyenne (on his mother's side). Kim Winona, of American Indian heritage, played the Indian maiden, Morning Star; Anthony Numkena, a Hopi Indian using the stage name Keena Nomkeena, played young Keena, the adopted son of Brave Eagle. Rounding out the regular cast was veteran comic, Bert Wheeler, as the halfbreed Smokey Joe (teller of tribal tall tales that also contained nuggets of wisdom).

The show effectively portrayed Native Americans not as savages, but as a civilized people who lived by their own well-structured societal rules. In each episode, young Keena learned a valuable "life lesson" from his father, Brave Eagle. A review in *TV Guide* noted, "CBS's *Brave Eagle* points up the Indian's basic dignity, moral values and way of life in a show with enough riding and shooting to please the most avid Western fan." Keith Larsen

147

once shared that the original concept of the show included a conscious effort to change the image of Indians: "We used to talk about that all the time. When you think about it, it was *their* country. We used to get letters from Navajos in Utah. We visited them and used a lot of their dialogue."

This image of Native Americans as a group of people who were courageously facing dramatic cultural change with dignity was front-and-center in the episodic storylines of the series. In the opening narrative to "The Challenge," Brave Eagle gave his perspective on the times:

> In a vast and cherished land of great beauty, we, the Cheyenne, lived as our ancestors had lived, teaching our young men and boys to understand the virtues of courage, of strength, and of honor. For in the youth rest the future of a people. Our wealth we counted in our fleet horses on which we followed the great herds of buffalo, from which came our meat, our clothing, and the skins for our teepees. When the white man crossed the plains, he brought with him a new way of life, and soldiers with 'fire sticks' to protect him. There was room for all in this bountiful land, and there were those among us who wished to live in peace with the paleface strangers and learn of their ways. But there were others whose lives were corrupted by the poison of hate. (*Brave Eagle*).

It was indeed a time of uncertainty for Native Americans in the West, and the chief sought to wisely guide his people through the changing times, with particular emphasis on educating his son, Keena, to be a wise future leader. The stories frequently centered on the theme of the struggle to reconcile one's traditions with new ideas. To Brave Eagle, it was a matter of maintaining and honoring one's heritage while also being willing to adapt to change: "For some of the old ways, it can only be said that they are old. For a wise man grows in wisdom with the seasons and forgets the old ways when new ways are better!"

Brave Eagle is mostly unknown to modern viewers – no surprise given its short run of only 26 episodes, all filmed in black and white. When the show originally aired on CBS, it was up against tough competition, *Disneyland*, on Wednesday nights. Rather than try another timeslot, CBS cancelled the show and replaced it with a new show, *Cartoon Theater*, featuring Dick Van Dyke.

Dale Evans, "Queen of the West"

While Dale Evans never had her own television series in the 1950s, she was a major B western star in her own right, as attested to by the use of her name and image in merchandising as well as her roles in movies, radio programs, and the *Roy Rogers* TV series. So it is worthwhile to take a brief look at this heroine, especially with regard to her serving as a role model.

Viewers and fans may debate whether Dale Evans was a sidekick or a heroine on *The Roy Rogers Show*, but nevertheless, her regular participation in Roy's adventures – and the independent nature of her character in the episodes – helped to distinguish the *Roy Rogers* series from the other B western shows on 1950s television. In *King of the Cowboys, Queen of the West*, the author Raymond E. White spoke highly of the unique role played by Dale in the TV show. "While Rogers, in that West, depicted himself as the stereotypical and romantic American cowboy with his six-gun, horse, and guitar, Dale Evans provided a more complex image," wrote White. "She played Roy's deferential sidekick, fitting the era's idea of women behind men. At the same time, she portrayed an independent heroine who often acted on her own. Her roles as a self-reliant woman set her apart from traditional western heroines and undoubtedly gave hope to her female fans that they could break out of the mold that American society defined for them."

Dale was also a featured character in juvenile western novels published during the years of the *Roy Rogers* series, as well as the lead character in her own comic book series! In the Little Golden Books series and other juvenile western books published by Whitman, Dale was depicted as a hero more-or-less equal to Roy. For example, in the Whitman book, *Roy Rogers and Dale Evans in River of Peril*, Dale at one point early in the story asserts, "I can handle a gun just as well as you can, Roy Rogers!" The story's narrative then elaborates with the commentary that "this was only a slight exaggeration. Roy could out-shoot her, firing at targets, but not by very much, just as he could outride and outrope her, but not by very much…" Later in the same book, after Dale and Trigger had acted to pull off a dramatic rescue of Roy from the perilous river, one of the book's main characters stated: "That's a horse in a million . . . and there's just nobody anywhere to equal Dale Evans!"

Dale had two comic book series during the television years. The first series was a DC series, "Queen of the Westerns," that ran through 1952 and 24 issues, and included photo covers on issues #1, 2, and 4-14. This series was followed by a Dell series, beginning with two 1953 issues in Dell's Four Color series. Beginning the regular series numbering with issue #3 (April-June 1954) and continuing through issue #22 (January-March 1959), Dell published "Queen of the West, DALE EVANS" – usually referred to more simply as DALE EVANS comics. The series included elements familiar to viewers of the *Roy Rogers* TV series: Pat Brady as her sidekick, along with his jeep, "Nellybelle," the dog, "Bullet," Dale's horse, "Buttermilk," and the operation by Dale of her own café in Mineral City.

Dale's status as a role model continued during and well after the 1950s. Over the years, Dale was a prolific author of inspirational books, including her best-seller, *Angel Unaware*. She and Roy were also featured as the hosts of several television programs and network specials, with Dale eventually hosting her own television talk-show. She recorded several solo albums of religious music, and over the years wrote many songs – including "Happy Trails" and "The Bible Tells Me So."

Aware of the public's attention to her (and Roy's) influence on children, Dale openly shared her perspectives on parenting. For example, she was quoted in an interview for a 1957 article in *Mirror*: "You can't tell a child, either, 'Benefit by my experience,' because that doesn't work. They want to try their own wings. It's best to instruct them under God. I teach them not to obey me for my sake, but for His sake. I tell them that Roy and I are just caretakers for Him, guarding His precious ones."

As a key part of the *Roy Rogers* TV series, Dale's character was, by default, associated with the tenets listed in the Roy Rogers Rider Club Rules. This was evident in the depiction of her characters, as well as in real life. Fittingly, her exhibit at the National Cowgirl Museum and Hall of Fame in Fort Worth, Texas, includes this quote from her: "'Cowgirl' is an attitude really. A pioneer spirit, a special American brand of courage. The cowgirl faces life head-on, lives by her own lights, and makes no excuses. Cowgirls take stands; they speak up. They defend things they hold dear."

Zorro

OPENING CREDITS: During a sequence of action scenes that includes sword-play, the theme song plays: "Out of the night when the full moon is bright, / comes a horseman known as Zorro / This bold renegade carves a "Z" with his blade / A "Z" that stands for Zorro / Zorro, Zorro, the fox so cunning and free / Zorro, Zorro, who makes the sign of the Z / Zorro, Zorro, Zorro, Zorro, Zorro, Zorro...." As the song ends, on screen is seen impressively silhouetted against the moon the image of Zorro, in his long cape, on a rearing Tornado.

The classic story featuring Don Diego De La Vega, a.k.a. "Zorro," the hero who leads a double life, came to life on television in 1957 on ABC. The TV show starred Guy Williams in the title role of Zorro, the hero who was the son of a wealthy California rancher by day, but the masked defender of the oppressed by night. Diego's (Zorro's) confidante and assistant, Bernardo, was played by Gene Sheldon. Bernardo was more-or-less Zorro's sidekick, who, unable to speak, communicated via sign language. Henry Calvin played Sergeant Garcia, a soldier who feels obligated to obey orders whether or not he agrees with the orders. The original broadcast of the series ended in 1959 after 78 episodes, all of which were produced by Walt Disney Productions, and sponsored on television by the Seven-Up Company.

Zorro came to television late in the 1950s, toward the end of the original productions of B western films-for-TV. Zorro had no written code by which he operated, but we include the show in this discussion for a couple of reasons. First, *Zorro* was immensely popular with children at the time and is still remembered fondly by them today. Secondly, even though he had no written code or creed, Zorro clearly acted in an ethical manner at all times, accomplishing his heroic feats within a framework of respect for the law and lawfully appointed authority figures, and without the violation of anyone's person or property.

As most of the injustice against which Zorro fought was caused by corrupt government officials in the Spanish-ruled Los Angeles of the 1820s, the need for him to act was usually easily understood by the young viewer. Also, the employment of story arcs that extended over many episodes made *Zorro* distinct in format from that of the other B westerns that had preceded it. This device also allowed for fuller development of certain storylines, making Zorro's fight for justice appear even more challenging since patience, persistence, and diligence were usually required in order to bring the bad guys to justice.

Daniel Boone

OPENING CREDITS: "Daniel Boone was a man, yes a big man! / With an eye like an eagle and as tall as a mountain was he / Daniel Boone was a man. Yes, a big man! / He was brave, he was fearless and as tough as a mighty oak tree! / From the coonskin cap on the top of ol' Dan to the heel of his rawhide shoe / The rippin'est, roarin'est, fightin'est man the frontier ever knew /Daniel Boone was a man. Yes, a big man / What a Boone, what a do-er, what a dream come-a true-er was he!"

Starring Fess Parker in the title role, *Daniel Boone* was an action/adventure series that aired on NBC from 1964 to 1970 for 165 hour-long episodes, all filmed in color after the first season. The series was set in time in the years surrounding and during the American Revolution, with the action centered mostly in the area around Boonesborough, Kentucky.

Fess Parker played the title role and was a co-owner of the series, capitalizing on the success he had with "King of the Wild Frontier," shown on television's *Disneyland*, in which he played the coonskin-cap wearing Davy Crockett. The incredible success of those broadcasts led to a merchandising bonanza which saw sales in the millions of items like: coonskin caps, toy "Old Betsy" muskets, buckskin shirts, T-shirts, coloring books, guitars, bath towels, bedspreads, wallets – anything with the Crockett name attached. A 2010 article in *TIME* magazine aptly described the cultural impact of Disney's *Crockett* films:

> Chances are, if you grew up in the mid-1950s, you either owned an official Davy Crockett coonskin cap or had the lyrics of the television show's theme song committed to memory: "Born on a mountaintop in Tennessee/ Greenest state in the land of the free ... Davy, Davy Crockett/ King of the wild frontier." Under the iconic cap — just one of the show's many merchandising tie-ins — stood Fess Parker, ... [the] Texas-born actor fit the rugged American frontiersman mold so well in the five Crockett episodes of ABC's *Disneyland* that he went on to play Daniel Boone in the 1960s NBC series of the same name. (*TIME*, April 5, 2010).

A very popular character in the *Daniel Boone* series was Daniel's faithful Indian companion, Mingo, played by actor Ed Ames. Mingo was an

Oxford-educated, part-Cherokee character who spoke perfect English, and – similar to Tonto – was a thoughtful, intelligent partner in Daniel's adventures.

Noteworthy for the themes of this book, is the fact that *Daniel Boone* was a series featuring a hero who was a family man! While the historical Daniel Boone had many children and the TV version only had two, the series was nonetheless distinct from other TV B westerns with its portrayal of an action hero who was a married man with children. Rebecca Boone, Daniel's wife, was played by Patricia Blair. Young son, Israel Boone, was played by Darby Hinton, and daughter Jemima (only seen in the first two seasons) was played by Veronica Cartwright.

A Sample of the lessons learned by Keena, as summarized by his father, Brave Eagle, in various episodes of *Brave Eagle*:

- "And thus it was Keena learned that the way of honor, while not always the easiest, is the surest path to travel; and the value of a man's word is the measure by which he is judged."

- An army colonel learned that "things are never as bad as they seemed" and Morning Star learned "that jealousy is an evil spirit that warps the reason," and "to his advantage, Keena learned at an early age that it is a woman's privilege to change her mind."

- "Thus, Keena's horizon became wider. He learned that one can make a mistake and still redeem himself with honesty, determination, and courage."

- "And thus it was that Keena learned that knowledge takes many forms, and that no one man can know all. For knowledge is dead when it is not given in the cause of good, and he gives most who uses his knowledge best."

- "...and Keena, who would one day be chief, learned that trickery defeats its own ends, but faith in a good cause provides the strength to defend that cause."

- "Keena learned that charm of manner and great skill do not alone deserve the hand of friendship. For a friend is he who gladly gives of himself for the good of his friend; but the man who demands that another suffer hardship for his own gain, is not a friend."

- "For the man who harbors revenge in his heart succeeds only in destroying himself."

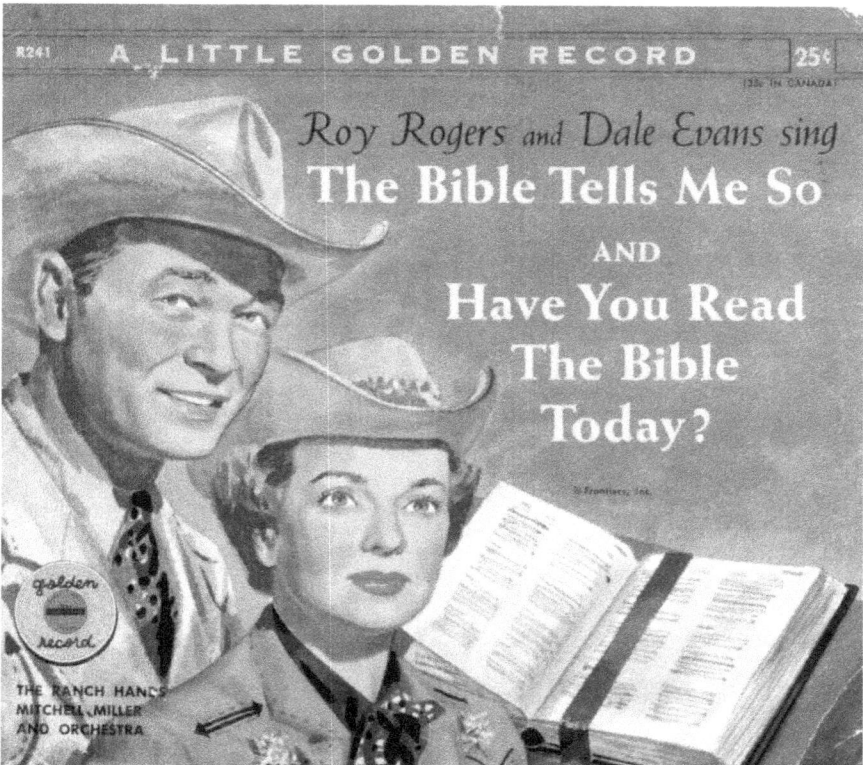

Dale Evans was a key part of the inspirational and religious-themed products for Roy Rogers, as illustrated by this album cover.

8

MERCHANDISING AND THE CODE

Most of our attention to this point has been on the connection between the on-screen personas of the B western heroes and their personal lives (at least as reported publicly) to the values expressed in their published codes and creeds. In this chapter, we will look at how the tie-in merchandising associated with these heroes also helped to further promote and reinforce the values expressed in their cowboy codes. However, we will begin by reviewing the sponsor's relationship with a show before considering the merchandising specifically.

"But First, Here's a Message from Our Sponsor..."

For television program sponsors, the goal was to advertise their product by reaching a targeted audience with their message. In television's infancy, many markets had only one or two stations serving a given area, and programming choices were correspondingly quite limited for most viewers. As a result, it was likely that most individuals had an awareness of the TV program(s) with which a particular sponsor was identified – whether or not they were a fan of that program. Thus, companies were quite selective in their choice of shows to sponsor.

Many modern readers will be unfamiliar with the degree to which early television advertising was influenced by the experiences of the radio industry. To get a clearer perspective for our brief discussion of early television programming sponsors, some historical context may be helpful. The shift in broadcasting emphasis from radio to television was a dramatic change for the culture, including the business world. Younger readers may gain at least some appreciation for this shift if compared with the changes observed by the initial advent of the internet-connected personal computer, and more recently, the increasing availability of on-demand, online streaming of programs.

In 1950, when barely five million television sets had been produced in the country, television was already succeeding in taking audiences away from their radios according to the Hooper ratings used commonly for radio programming at the time. The March 27, 1950 issue of *Quick* magazine reported: "The first Hooper report on combined radio-TV ratings in New York showed that of the top 15 shows, nine were TV shows."

This long-anticipated, but new, medium of television was catching on rapidly. By the end of 1950, industry surveys showed that nearly 18% of U.S. families owned a television set, with about half of them concentrated in just five markets (New York, Los Angeles, Chicago, Philadelphia, and Boston). By the following year, television was attracting sponsors away from radio to the extent that radio shows were becoming something of a bargain for sponsors as radio attempted to lure back some of those advertising dollars.

Change came rather quickly for advertising within the broadcast industry. By the end of 1951, television was rapidly expanding to become the dominant media form, making it a cultural force in advertising power. In the U.S., there were 108 TV stations, with an estimated 14 million TV sets in existence – up from about three million sets in 1949. By the middle of 1953, sponsors were advised they could reach some 11 million TV homes – about 52% of all the TV homes in the U.S. at the time – simply by concentrating their business on just nine television stations in nine U.S. cities! (The stations cited were: WNBT New York, WNBQ Chicago, KNBH Los Angeles, WPTZ Philadelphia, WBZ-TV Boston, WNBK Cleveland, WNBW Washington, D. C., WRGB Schenectady -Albany -Troy, and KPTV Portland, Ore.) As the power of television advertising was discovered, sponsors quickly transitioned their advertising spend dollars to television following the same business model used in radio: underwriting specific shows and programs.

Reaching Parents Through What the Kids Would Watch

Television advertisers immediately applied lessons already learned in the radio industry, one of which was that the juvenile audience was a gateway to capturing the whole family audience. Radio advertisers had already discovered that parents listened to the programs their kids wanted to hear, and thus, commercials that apparently were aimed at the youngsters were actually designed to catch the attention of the adults in the room. Radio sponsors for children's adventure shows (*Dick Tracy*, *Terry and the Pirates*, *Superman*, *Captain Midnight*, etc.) included cereals (Quaker Oats, Kellogg's Corn Flakes, Ralston), as well as bakers (Ward Baking), drinks (Ovaltine), and Peter Pan Peanut Butter, along with bread and milk companies.

This successful advertising scheme was also applied to western programming, with cowboy adventures heavily subsidized by companies like General Mills, General Foods, Interstate Bakeries, and National Biscuit Company. In a 1954 article in the industry publication, *Sponsor*, advertisers were reminded of the prime opportunity represented by sponsorship of juvenile western programming:

> James Stewart was once quoted regarding the value of capturing a family audience. "A good Western will always appeal to a family audience," he says, "and I think it is important for our industry to concentrate on making films which have an appeal for the whole family. I do feel that there are enough clean stories and ideas to keep me busy from now on. I always want to be in a picture which parents will bring their kids to see."
>
> Stewart was speaking of theater films, but felt the same about TV westerns. He also felt the small screen of television to be a handicap since it was more difficult to visually convey the big, open space character of the West.
>
> ("What I Look for in a Western" by James Stewart , from *Western Stars of Television and Film*, edited by Ken and Sylvia Ferguson, 1967, Purnell.)

A biscuit company may want to sell both sweet goods and salted crackers on television. Since children are mainly responsible for the brand of cookies their mothers buy, a program like *Hopalong Cassidy* reaches the right audience. This kind of program would, in effect, be double-barreled, since statistics show that about half of Hoppy's audience is adult and the biscuit company could get across its salted-cracker message on the same show. (*Sponsor*, April 5, 1954).

The network programming folks also figured out that it was to their advantage to capture the youthful audience with their early evening shows. A 1955 industry report concluded that TV sets tuned into juvenile programming on a given station, were more likely to remain tuned to that station for its later evening programming. As an example of this strategy, the report cited the decisions by ABC's programmers: "ABC got the drift and the edge by putting "Disneyland" in at 7:30 (EST). Its composition of audience, like that of *The Lone Ranger* and *Rin Tin Tin*, is family – kids plus adults. Lots of viewers per set. Good climate for advertising." The same article reported that NBC would soon likely be making changes, given the fact that "the kiddies swing the family from *Roy Rogers* on NBC to *Lassie* on CBS where they stay right through *Private Secretary* and *Ed Sullivan* (until they are forced to go to bed)." (*Sponsor*, April 18, 1955). Clearly, pursuing the loyalty of the young audience was in the best interests of networks and advertisers.

Local businesses were able to take advantage of the new opportunities presented by television program advertising, as well. In 1951, an Atlanta business, Prior Tire, sponsored the half-hour, Saturday afternoon broadcast of *Hopalong Cassidy*. During one Saturday commercial it was stated that children accompanied by their parents to one of their stores could obtain a combination package of Hopalong Cassidy buttons and a pistol. The sponsor had pre-purchased 2,500 of these packages, and "by Tuesday, they were all out of buttons and pistols, and their store was jammed." (*Sponsor*, November 5, 1951).

Thus, we can see how this advertising strategy of reaching parents through juvenile programming began with radio, but was very quickly established as common wisdom for television. By September, 1949, *Sponsor* magazine noted in an article, "TV Captures the Kids," that:

about one out of every three programs seen on the visual network air today is a show aimed squarely at the juvenile audience. Almost 75% of them are sponsored. In addition to this line-up, a growing list of both affiliated and independent TV stations is devoting increasing time and programing efforts toward building good juvenile shows. Again, more than 60% of them are sponsored. (*Sponsor*, September 26, 1949).

For the sponsor, the "message" was all about advertising their products, and their identification with a juvenile television program enabled them to build brand recognition as never before. By late 1949, the potential of TV advertising was being recognized throughout the industry: "Sponsor identification reaches heights in juvenile shows never touched by radio. Brand loyalties, something that radio at all times found difficult to establish in the fickle juvenile field, are much stronger. Program ratings on a well-planned TV kid show are invariably above average, sometimes reaching top-bracket popularity levels." (*Sponsor*, September 26, 1949).

In a 1953 study, breakfast cereal brands were seen to be very successful with their TV sponsorships. The report included this observation: "The greatest degree of program identification was scored by the Post Tens buyers, 81 per cent of whom saw the brand advertised on *Roy Rogers*. Of the Post Toasties buyers, 76 per cent had seen it on *Captain Video*." (*Television Magazine*, April, 1953).

There was abundant evidence in the industry that the cowboy hero was a popular – and profitable – programming choice for advertisers. For example, in mid-1950, the Bobby Benson name, from March to May of that year, reportedly sold over $300,000 worth of merchandise – just in Macy's stores! That same year, Hopalong Cassidy-endorsed products were selling at a pace to reach an estimated $20 million.

The sponsors operating on a national scale were not the only beneficiaries of the western television advertising bonanza. Local sponsors found it a lucrative opportunity as well. A good example of this is from the Giant Food Department stores successful sponsorship of Pick Temple in the Washington, D.C., television market. Given the prevailing craze among youngsters for western heroes in the early 1950s, Giant wanted to sponsor a cowboy star as a way to increase their bread sales. They could have chosen one of the nationally known stars - considering the successful marketing already associated with some bread competitors (for example, Sunshine bread and Gene Autry, County Fair bread and the Cisco Kid, and Bond bread and Hopalong Cassidy) – to sponsor on a local basis. However, Giant chose to sponsor 12 hours weekly of the local television cowboy program, the *Pick Temple Show,* on WTOP-TV. They chose Mr. Temple because he was already identified with the local community, popular in the area, available for frequent personal appearances locally, and because of "his uniquely-shaped cowboy personality which stresses the good behavior of children that concerned parents try to impress upon their offspring."

The choice of a local cowboy hero personality paid off handsomely for Giant. The store knew that children are always delighted to see their favorite stars in person, and was able to make Mr. Temple accessible to them through many local personal appearance opportunities. Even better for Giant was the fact that most of such personal appearances could be tied to show-related merchandising campaigns. Giant's bread sales in early 1953 were an insignificant percentage of the total bread sales in the Washington market, where only three competitor brands – Wonder, Bond, and Wright's – combined for about a 60% market share. However, in Giant's stores, their Giant-branded bread outsold all other breads at the rate of three to one! By March, 1953, Giant was planning to build six new stores to expand their already-existing chain of 24 stores in the metropolitan D.C. area.

An additional factor in the success of juvenile television program sponsorships was that the target audience is not a static group, but constantly refreshing. Young fans were constantly growing in and out of the target age group, providing sponsors with a fresh audience to which they could appeal. This was especially important for sponsors interested in advertising spots for TV shows appearing only in re-runs. The *Roy Rogers Show,* for example, was highly successful for Nestle when it went into syndication as re-runs. By March of 1959, Nestle was sponsoring the show in 88 cities, giving the show exposure that was equal to some network line-ups! Significant to Nestle was the fact that the re-runs-only status of the show appeared "to make little difference in children's programs since there's virtually an entirely new generation of young viewers every season or two." (*Sponsor*, March 28, 1959).

Tie-in Merchandising

Television shows targeting a juvenile audience – and especially the B westerns – immediately discovered a lucrative market for the selling of program-related merchandise. By late 1949, the advertising industry had taken note of the sales potential of this new programming medium. "Nearest and dearest to the hearts of advertisers and agencies, however, are the sales and promotional results brought in by juvenile shows in TV, which in some cases have sent sales curves skyrocketing and have had dealers excitedly re-ordering merchandise that has moved faster than ever before," reported *Sponsor* magazine in September, 1949.

Sales of promotional items served to boost the popularity of the western stars while also building a measure of loyalty to the program, and there was no shortage of items from which to choose for the youngsters wishing to have a product endorsed by their favorite hero. Tie-in merchandising was a win-win-win for the B western show producers, retailers, and the audience. For the young fans making up the viewing audience, it provided a tangible way for them to continue to enjoy their favorite program. For the retailers, it was an opportunity to sell a product in high demand, resulting in increased traffic to their stores. But for the producers of the B westerns, it was a necessary revenue stream that enabled their shows to get on the air in the first place.

The industry quickly discovered that producing television programs was an expensive venture. (Some have commented on the move from radio to television in this context, noting that radio was a superior form of story-telling and much cheaper to produce, as it was not bound by all the limitations – both physical and budgetary – involved in providing a visual representation of the story.) The production of a TV cowboy show was even more expensive, costing some 25% to 35% more to produce than the cost of other dramatic shows. Since sponsors were unwilling to pay more to sponsor a western, the ability to market tie-in products was critical to a cowboy show's financial success.

To illustrate this financial aspect of the business and the corresponding importance of merchandising income to a show, consider the example of Flying A Productions, as reported in a 1956 article in *Broadcasting*. Producing western action programming was more expensive due to several factors. Straight dramatic shows could often be totally filmed on a sound stage without any travel costs, but the westerns usually required a major portion of their filming to occur on location. That meant the incurring of additional expenses like transportation for the cast and crew, hotel bills, trucking fees, and much more – plus overtime pay for time spent in traveling to and from the remote locations. In addition, there were expenses uniquely associated with filming a western program: rental, care and feeding of livestock; salaries of the wranglers who handle the animals; and time lost through bad weather and sound interference from air and highway traffic. All of these combined to add to the production costs for a show that must compete for airtime with shows produced more cheaply. Fortunately for the production companies, tie-in products could be very profitable. In 1956, the estimated gross income for Flying A Productions was $59 million, of which $46 million was generated from merchandising tie-ins.

Long before television, the earnings potential for western stars who had merchandise license agreements with manufacturers was recognized with the success of Tom Mix premiums promoted by the Ralston Cereal Company. Other western stars then followed with successful merchandise programs of their own, including the Lone Ranger, Gene Autry, and Red Ryder. With the advent of television broadcasting, the TV cowboy stars found immediate financial success in merchandising, and the manufacture of tie-in products for a western hero became a foregone conclusion as soon as a new show hit the air: "By fall, *Wild Bill Hickok* should be stampeding

A 1950 *TIME* magazine article described how the popularity of TV's western programs had changed the playtime activities of children: "Overnight, almost every little boy & girl in the nation had become a cowboy." Expanding on the extent of television's impact, the article noted that even though children had played in the world of Old West make-believe previously, what was different was their demand for manufactured toys and clothes:

> Children with impressively styled cap guns and bejeweled double holsters (many tied to their thighs to facilitate a fast draw) were so commonplace that those without them seemed a little underdressed, and those who still carried such outmoded armament as X-Ray Guns or Atomic Disintegrators, hopelessly old fashioned.

("MANNERS & MORALS: Kiddies in the Old Corral", *TIME*, Nov. 27, 1950) the air waves, radio and TV. And it probably won't be too long after that that he'll be in the movies and comic books." (*Sponsor*, July 17, 1950).

With the rise of juvenile programming on television, retailers began to reap immediate rewards through the sale of tie-in merchandise. Even while experiencing a slump in sales of other items, retailers reported sales of cowboy clothes and items had actually surged. Whenever one of the western stars made a personal appearance at a retail location, the retailers cashed in as never before. One such occasion was described by a *TIME* reporter in 1949:

> As a hard-riding, straight-shooting cowboy, William ("Hopalong Cassidy") Boyd has been the star of dozens of B movies. Last week, as Cowboy Boyd strode into New Orleans' D. H. Holmes department store, the fanfare would have done justice to a Technicolored A production. He was there to plug his Hopalong Cassidy boots, spurs, shirts, toy guns and some 37 other cowboy items for moppets, and 50,000 fans and customers were on hand to say howdy. (*TIME*, August 29, 1949).

By early 1952, children were reportedly reading less than they did before having a television set in their home. However, they also reported they continued to read as many comic books as they read prior to having television. Comic books of various western stars sold millions of copies every month, with Dell printing lengthy runs for its Lone Ranger, Roy Rogers, and Gene Autry titles. Juvenile novels and story books were also printed and sold in huge numbers. For example, the popular Little Golden Books series had top-selling titles in the mid-1950s featuring such TV show characters as Roy Rogers, and the Lone Ranger.

Merchandising and the Cowboy Code

For the purposes of this book, our primary interest lies in the question of whether the merchandising of tie-in products in any way reinforced the values expressed in the various cowboy codes and creeds. With a focus again on the "big 4," let us now consider the successful promotion of their merchandise and any observable connections to their published cowboy codes.

Hopalong Cassidy

William Boyd was labelled by some as the King of the Cowboy Merchandisers, a reference to how Hopalong Cassidy merchandise exploded on the market with his move to television. As noted by radio historian Dunning:

> His endorsement for any product meant instant sales in the millions. It meant overnight shortages, frantic shopping sprees, and millions of dollars for Boyd. There were Hopalong Cassidy bicycles, roller skates (complete with spurs), Hoppy pajamas, Hopalong beds. The demand for Hoppy shirts and pants was so great that a shortage of black dye resulted. (Dunning, *On the Air – The Encyclopedia of Old-Time Radio*).

Boyd occasionally addressed the youthful audience in his episode trailers to encourage their purchase of Hopalong products. In a trailer used with a couple of episodes, and following the sponsor's commercial at the end of the episode, Hopalong had this personal message for the kids: "Hi there! Did you hear what the man said? I did - and I agree with every word of it. If you buy his product, I'm sure you'll like it – and it'll tickle my sponsor to death." (Trailer #2, *Hopalong Cassidy* television series). In the trailer used with some other episodes, Hopalong assured the kids – or perhaps the parents – about the quality of the Hoppy-branded merchandise: "I would just like to assure you that any product you see Hoppy's name on, in my mind, is the finest." (Trailer #5, *Hopalong Cassidy* television series).

Unlike Disney, who targeted ages two to ten with his merchandising, Boyd targeted older children who could already read and write. As Hopalong Cassidy author Harry L. Rinker told it, Boyd targeted the seven to fourteen age group for his products. Boyd "wanted a vocal market, a market where his followers could verbally tell their parents, 'I want one of those.'" His strategy worked, as kids across the U.S. bombarded their parents with requests for anything Hoppy-related.

The third article in Hopalong Cassidy's "Creed for American Boys and Girls," states: "If you want to be respected, you must respect others. Show good manners in every way." This principle was underscored in a story appearing in an April, 1950, Fawcett comic book story, "The Land Grabbers," featuring Hopalong Cassidy as a sheriff. In this story, Polecat was the leader of the bad guys who were planning to shoot the men of an Indian tribe, the Taconda, who were then living on an Indian reservation outside of Twin River, and take over their land. Polecat tells Hoppy, "This looks like good grazing land so my friends and me decided tuh settle down hyar and raise cattle!"

Hoppy responds, "What do you mean you decided to settle down here? This land belongs to the Taconda tribe!"

Polecat answers, "I know! We gave them a chance tuh move on peacefully, but when they refused, we were gonna shoot them! After all, they're only injuns!"

Hoppy then points his finger in the man's face, saying, "Only Indians! Look here, Indians are as good as anybody else, and they're not only entitled to the same privileges but as long as I'm sheriff here, they're going to get them!"

In partnership with Bond bread, Hopalong Cassidy published a second 10-point creed, this one titled, "Hopalong Cassidy's Creed for School Children." This creed consisted of ten articles printed on a textbook cover for the use of young students with their school textbooks. Interestingly, this cover itself provided a practical means of implementing the first article (keeping textbooks in good condition) of this creed. The ten articles are as follows:

1. Remember your desk and textbooks will have to be used by the next class. Keep your desk and books in good condition.
2. Fire and air raid drills are for your safety. Pay attention and follow all orders quickly and quietly.
3. Neatness counts in both your dress and work. Keep a neat appearance and be careful in your penmanship. Sloppy work will show up on your report card.
4. School lunchrooms are clean and pleasant. Eat quietly and try to leave your place as clean as you found it.
5. Traffic rules are for the benefit of all. Do not run in the corridors. Obey the instructions of all teachers and monitors.
6. Punctuality and attendance are very important. Arrive on time and try not to miss any classes unless it is absolutely necessary.
7. Nobody likes a cheat. You'll feel better, and do better, if the work you hand in is your own.
8. Good grades require doing the proper amount of homework.

Together with your parents, you can work out a plan that will give you time for play and study.

9. Teachers play a vital role in our nation. They are there to help you become a good citizen. They will appreciate it if you are courteous and helpful.

10. Be proud of your school. You'll enjoy it a lot more if you take part in at least one of the many sports and activities your school offers.

Gene Autry

Merchandising of Gene Autry products had been going on for years prior to his ever appearing on television. As with Hopalong Cassidy, following the airing of his programs on television, demand for Gene Autry items skyrocketed. Like his fellow cowboy heroes, Gene Autry merchandise always promoted the same positive, role-model image seen in his on-screen performances, and traits consistent with his cowboy Code of the West.

Gene Autry has been called "America's Favorite Singing Cowboy" by some folks, given his prolific success in musical recordings. His first recording, "Silver-Haired Daddy," was made in 1930, and reportedly had sold five million copies by 1951. Gene went on to record some two dozen songs that charted well on the Billboard Singles Sales Chart. Other than "Back in the Saddle Again," he is probably more known today for his Christmas-themed hits that charted on Billboard during the early television days: "Here Comes Santa Claus," (in 1947 and 1948), "Rudolph, the Red-Nosed Reindeer" (in 1949, 1950 and 1951), and "Frosty The Snowman" (in 1950 and 1951). Another holiday favorite was "Here Comes Peter Cottontail," charting on Billboard in 1950 and 1951.

In 1951, fan magazine *Radio and Television Mirror* promoted a contest involving Gene Autry's code of conduct. The magazine stated that "looking and living the part of a cowboy isn't enough. A fearless, honest cowboy has high ideals. No matter what the circumstances, he has the courage to stick by his code." Under the contest title, "Gene Autry Prize Round-Up," boys and girls were invited to submit drawings depicting Gene Autry – and his horse, Champion, if they wished – acting out one of his "Code of the West" rules. The contest was open to boys and girls up to the age of twelve, and entries were judged according to age by Gene and the magazine's editors. The rules required the drawings to be on a paper about eight by eleven inches, and could be colored with crayons, water colors, or whatever the artist chose. Judging of the entries was based on "originality and imagination in capturing the spirit of Gene Autry and his Code of the West, according to the contestant's age." Winners were announced in a later issue of the magazine, with prizes awarded, including: 1st prizes – a Gene Autry Monark Bicycle; 2nd and 3rd prizes – The Gene Autry Six-Shooter Watch; 4th and 5th prizes – a Gene Autry Gun and Holster Set; and the next eighteen prizes – a Gene Autry Electric Pencil.

Roy Rogers

He was not the first cowboy star to offer tie-in merchandise, neither was he the first cowboy star to have wild success with such merchandising, but in the end, Roy Rogers was arguably the leader in tie-in product sales – both in the vast array of merchandise produced and overall sales volume – among the cowboy heroes. "From the middle 1940s until the mid-1950s, Roy had approximately 400 merchandising articles - everything from lunch pails to cap pistols - with his name on them. Roy was second only to Walt Disney in commercial tie-ups," noted author David Rothel (Rothel, *The Roy Rogers Book*).

Throughout the 1950s, retail sales of Roy's merchandise reportedly averaged $30 million annually! The well-known Double-R-Bar brand had appeared on "cap guns, hats, pajamas, boots, holster sets, lunch boxes, pocketknives, and so many other items (400 products total) that at one point the Sears Catalogue devoted 12 pages to Roy Rogers products." (O'Neal, *American Cowboy*). Roy's picture had been on the front of an estimated 2 ½ billion boxes of Post Cereals (his long-time sponsor on both radio and television), and Roy appeared in various other advertisements and television commercials throughout the 1950s and 1960s for products ranging from hot chocolate to Chevrolet trucks.

Some of the tie-in merchandising offered opportunities for the same kind of moralizing that was experienced in the television series, and served to underscore the values expressed in the Riders Club Rules. This was especially true of print items like comic books and Whitman-published novels. For example, in the Whitman novel, *Roy Rogers and Dale Evans in River of Peril*, there are at least three occasions in which a "moral point" is made for the juvenile reader. The premise of this story is that Roy has willingly accepted a dangerous assignment from the President of the United

States because: "When the President of the United States asked for a job to be undertaken, nobody had the right to do any refusing." After the story's main bad guy, Mayo Morgan, complains that his fellow outlaws were "a bunch of scary chicken-heads" because they had deserted him during a fight that was not going well for them, Roy replies: "That's the sort you usually get stuck with, the kind of business you're in."

Later, after Roy and friends had successfully faced and overcome some difficult challenges, the narrative states: "...Roy had always held firmly to two beliefs – one, that a man could do about anything if he set his mind to it; and two, that the worst sin of life was to back away from a problem, any problem, and not tackle it with every bit of determination possible. Failure was preferable to not even trying."

Dell Comics produced a lengthy Roy Rogers comic book series featuring Roy and Trigger in action-packed adventure stories. The monthly comic book was selling at the rate of 1,300,000 per issue in 1948 – *before* Roy was on television! The comic books also offered a chance to further enhance the family man image of Roy Rogers with some issues including entire pages devoted to reports on life within the Rogers family. In other issues, a "Roy's Mail Box" feature permitted Roy to weigh in on topics about which readers had submitted questions – from one's proper attitude toward strict teachers to when is it okay to take the Lord's name in vain.

For Roy (and Dale), the connection to the values in the Riders Club Rules was also observable in the forms of recorded music and via the books authored by Dale. Together, Roy and Dale recorded several audio albums that accompanied children's story books – some of them religious-themed. The two also performed together on numerous recordings of religious music, though mostly well after *The Roy Rogers Show*'s initial network run.

Throughout the years after his television show aired, Roy was increasingly open about his faith – an article included explicitly in the Riders Club Rules – in public appearances. Even during personal appearances in the 1950s, it was common for Roy to remind the kids in the audience that "it was not sissy to go to Sunday School or to say prayers at bedtime. Then with Trigger kneeling in imitation of humans in prayer, Roy would sing an inspirational song such as 'Peace in the Valley'." (Rothel, *The Roy Rogers Book*).

The Lone Ranger

A few months after the broadcast debut in 1933 of *The Lone Ranger* radio program, the show's producers at radio station WXYZ decided to offer the first *Lone Ranger* premium over the air. The response they received would also serve as a measure of the size of the listening audience. On the May 16, 1933 broadcast, a popgun was offered and the station prepared itself to process 1,000 requests. They were overwhelmed with almost 25,000 requests, and the Lone Ranger himself had to ask for relief on the air! Other merchandise was offered in the years following, and tie-in merchandising for the *Lone Ranger* was already going strong well before the television program.

Comic books and juvenile novels were sold by the millions and provided stories that captured the essence of the values written in the Lone Ranger Creed, at times doing so rather explicitly. Some Lone Ranger comic book stories appealed to one's patriotism and pride in our nation's heritage. For example, in the Gold Key Giant Comic issue, *The Lone Ranger Golden West*, No. 1, is a story titled, "He Finds Dan Reid." At the end of this story is this conversational exchange between the Lone Ranger and young Dan Reid:

LONE RANGER: Grandma Frisby was a fine woman, Dan! She and your father left you a great heritage!

DAN: A heritage?

LONE RANGER: Yes! They and others like them have handed down to you the right to worship as you choose; and the right to work and profit from your enterprise! They have given you a land where there is true freedom – true equality of opportunity! A nation that is governed by the people – by laws that are best for the greatest number! Your duty, Dan, is to preserve that heritage and strengthen it! That is the duty of every American!

DAN: I'll do all I can! I-I've got a lot to live up to because my uncle is The Lone Ranger!

The Lone Ranger and Tonto were so popular, that Dell also published a series featuring Tonto as the main hero. The stories in these comics continued to underscore the same values promoted in the Lone Ranger Creed. For example, consider the two stories in *The Lone Ranger's Companion Tonto* issue No. 19, published in 1955. The first story in this issue is "War

Trail," in which Stone Bear recounts the story of how Tonto once performed a heroic deed for his tribe. He concludes by telling Tonto: "When we returned to our council fire, we spoke of your deed! How you rode off alone rather than slow down our party – teaching us that there are times when one must sacrifice his own safety for the safety of the greater number!" As Tonto rides away, Stone Bear adds: "It is good to renew memories of brave deeds, Tonto! They inspire others to act wisely!" Stone Bear's summary was a direct reference to article #7 in the Lone Ranger's creed: "That men should live by the rule of what is best for the greatest number."

In the second story within that comic book issue, "Army Scout," Tonto helped recover stolen cavalry horses while dealing with an army sergeant who believes all Indians are liars. At the end, after he has learned how he was wrong to hold such opinions, he told his commanding officer: "I'd not be riding back with our horses, sir, if it wasn't for Tonto! I owe him an apology – and all Indians an apology!"

The sergeant continued: "He taught me it's wrong to suspect a whole group of people because they look different from you! There are good Indians and a few bad ones – just as there are good and bad white men! And any time Tonto wants to act as Army Scout for my outfit, I'll be proud to draw rein with him!" (dialogue in "Army Scout," *The Lone Ranger's Companion Tonto*, May-July, 1955).

This moral-to-the-story reminded readers of article #2 of the Lone Ranger's creed, "That all men are created equal and that everyone has within himself the power to make this a better world."

The relationship of the Lone Ranger and Tonto as equal partners in the fight against injustice was a key element of *The Lone Ranger* – especially in the television series. This partnership was also on display in the tie-in merchandising. A fine example of this is seen in the Little Golden Book title, *The Lone Ranger and Tonto*. On the final page of the story, an elementary school teacher addressed her class. "Now, children," she said, "We'll try spelling. Does anyone know how to spell hero?" In the illustration on the page, a boy and girl are both shown writing their responses on the chalkboard. The boy wrote "Lone Ranger," while the girl wrote "Tonto." The teacher simply smiled and said, "You're both right."

Tapping into the patriotic reputation of the Lone Ranger, the U.S. Treasury Department partnered with the Lone Ranger in 1958 to promote a campaign for the sale of U.S. Savings Stamps among America's young people through the organization of a "Peace Patrol." The campaign included gift books and a 25-cent Savings Stamp with an American flag design, and was the most intensive such campaign the Treasury Department had undertaken since World War II, according to a *TV Guide* article in October, 1958.

From the National Archives one can view the promotional film used for the Lone Ranger Peace Patrol, featuring Clayton Moore in character as the Lone Ranger speaking about the campaign. The film follows the Lone Ranger as he visits various national monuments and important sites around Washington, D.C., and meets dignitaries like Vice President Richard Nixon, Postmaster General Arthur Summerfield, and James F. Stiles, the Director of the Savings Bond Division. In the film's introduction, Moore – as the Lone Ranger – began with these words: "Hello, friends. Over the years you've shared my adventures on the side of law, order and peace in the exciting days of the old west. This time I want you to go along on a real life, present day adventure in the cause of world peace."

Other television show characters had earlier participated in similar campaigns, including Mister Ed, a 1954 Stamp Day for Superman, a 1957 "Leave It to Beaver U.S. Savings Bond Promotion," and Lassie (in support of the Lone Ranger's Peace Patrol in 1958). For the Lone Ranger, it was another way of living out articles #6 ("That 'this government, of the people, by the people, and for the people,' shall live always") and #10 ("I believe in my Creator, my country, my fellow man") of the Lone Ranger's creed.

In this page from a Christmas story appearing in a December, 1956, issue of *March of Comics* featuring Roy Rogers, Roy deflects praise away from himself by quoting from the Bible.

Dear Roy:
I'll bet there are always a lot of new animals on a ranch like yours. Do you have any new horses? I love horses.

Jimmy E.—Indianapolis

Dear Jimmy:
Yes, we have. Last fall, some people in Pennsylvania gave us a palomino pony. He looks like a small-sized Trigger, so we've named him "Tiny Trigger."

Your friend,

Roy Rogers

Dear Roy:
What is the best exercise for a boy? I am 12 years old, and some of my friends go in for weight-lifting.

Jerry S.—Los Angeles

Dear Jerry:
I think you are a little young for weight-lifting. You'd better ask your doctor. I believe that swimming, hiking, running, and other exercises your gym teacher will tell you about are best.

Your friend,

Roy Rogers

Dear Roy:
Isn't it all right to say cuss words when you're real mad?

Floyd J.—St. Louis

Dear Floyd:
It is never all right to take the Lord's name in vain.

Your friend,

Roy Rogers

Dear Roy:
What should I do to get along with my teacher? He's so bossy.

Carl E.—New Haven

Dear Carl:
Just about the best friend I have in the world today is the school teacher I once thought was too "bossy." When I began to do what he suggested, I found out he wasn't bossy—just strict and sensible. He helped me get started raising a pig for the 4-H Club. I won a prize, and that started my whole career.
You'll get along fine with your teacher if you remember that he's being strict for your own good—so you'll learn the things you need to know to become a good adult citizen.

Your friend,

Roy Rogers

Dear Roy:
How old is Trigger? I have heard that you don't have the real Trigger any more. How much did you pay for him, and when did you get him?

Frank R.—San Francisco

Dear Frank:
Trigger is 27 years old. I still have the original Trigger on the Double-R-Bar Ranch. I bought him in 1938 for $2,500, and it was the best money I ever spent.

Your friend,

Roy Rogers

Roy Rogers provided sound advice in this page from the July-August, 1960, issue of the Dell comic title, *Roy Rogers and Trigger*.

NO WONDER

THE YOUNGER SET

LOVES TV

Mother Goose certainly has had to take a back seat to Davy Crockett and other television characters in the past year. Nowhere is the impact more evident than in the realm of toys and costumes designed for the younger set. Some of the more popular outfits and accessories, available coast to coast, are, left to right: Pinky Lee get-up, with TV camera; Superman, with muscle-building set; Ramar of the Jungle, complete with gun and stuffed tiger; Gene Autry boots, vest, chaps, hat and guitar; Davy Crockett

20

Tie-in merchandising for several popular heroes were featured in this article in the October 8, 1955, issue of *TV Guide*, including products for western

Toys from Toy Manufacturers of the U.S.A., Inc.

dress for girls (in brown), with Annie Oakley sewing kit. Then there's the blue Annie Oakley costume, with white smoke-gun; Tinkerbell dress and Tinkerbell doll; Donald Duck outfit; Clarabell, with a *Howdy Doody* beach ball, and Dale Evans costume, with rocking horse. Many basic outfits, which will turn any little boy or girl into a reasonable facsimile of a TV idol, can be bought for about $2. It's the accessories—just as in the more adult automobile business—that run the price up.

21

heroes Gene Autry, Davy Crockett, Annie Oakley, and Dale Evans. ("No Wonder the Younger Set Loves TV." *TV Guide*, October 8, 1955.)

Hopalong Cassidy's Creed for School Children

1. Remember your desk and textbooks will have to be used by the next class. Keep your desk and books in good condition.

2. Fire and air raid drills are for your safety. Pay attention and follow all orders quickly and quietly.

3. Neatness counts in both your dress and work. Keep a neat appearance and be careful in your penmanship. Sloppy work will show up on your report card.

4. School lunchrooms are clean and pleasant. Eat quietly and try to leave your place as clean as you found it.

5. Traffic rules are for the benefit of all. Do not run in the corridors. Obey the instructions of all teachers and monitors.

6. Punctuality and attendance are very important. Arrive on time and try not to miss any classes unless it is absolutely necessary.

7. Nobody likes a cheat. You'll feel better, and do better, if the work you hand in is your own.

8. Good grades require doing the proper amount of homework. Together with your parents, you can work out a plan that will give you time for play and study.

9. Teachers play a vital role in our nation. They are there to help you become a good citizen. They will appreciate it if you are courteous and helpful.

10. Be proud of your school. You'll enjoy it a lot more if you take part in at least one of the many sports and activities your school offers.

FOR HEALTHY BODIES AND HAPPY HEARTS —

EAT *Bond Bread*

This is part of a book cover that was a Bond Bread tie-in merchandising item that students could use for their school textbooks. It contained yet another 10-item Creed from Hopalong Cassidy.

This panel with dialogue from the story, "He Finds Dan Reid," referenced multiple points of the Lone Ranger's Creed. The story appeared in the October, 1966, Gold Key Giant comic, *The Lone Ranger Golden West*.

9

A CODE TO LIVE BY

In the 1950s, it was still possible for children to interact with a generation that had taken part in the settling of the Old West. In April, 1951, a story in *Quick* reported on how a young audience listened spellbound to the recollections of Indian fighter Ed Ryan, then aged 94, telling about his escape from death during Custer's Last Stand (which had occurred 76 years prior). Modern readers can easily miss the fact that during television's infancy (1949-1951), such opportunities to personally meet and learn from real-life Old West participants was still possible (for example, Laura Ingalls Wilder lived until early 1957), not to mention surviving family members in some cases. Unfortunately, the folks who lived during the time of the Old West have all now passed on, leaving only their legacy for today's readers.

With the passing of those generations, some of whom qualified as "heroes," the question some have since posed is whether our current culture still needs heroes. And, if so, who qualifies as a "hero"? Once a hero has been identified as such, how does that hero determine the 'right thing' for which to fight?

Who Gets To Make The Rules?

An essay appearing in *TIME* magazine in 1966 explored the question, "Does the U.S. need heroes?" The author observed:

Even the U.S.'s most sacrosanct heroes have a relation to American life that is not quite equivalent to other nations' heroes. Britain's Wellington, France's Napoleon, Russia's Peter the Great are national heroes, who specifically did something for the greater glory of the nation and can be claimed by no other country. But the U.S.'s Washington and Lincoln, Wilson and Kennedy are celebrated for the ideals they championed. They reaffirm the American idea of itself as

Clayton Moore, television's Lone Ranger, believed in the power of Western film to impart values:

But I can't help but long for a real return to the Western. Westerns are true Americana. They tell of the struggles of our ancestors who came West seeking new homes, new ways of living, freedom and the promise of a bright future. The story of the West is inspiring and terrible, idealistic and bloody, sublime and atrocious. It embodies this country's best and worst characteristics. The good parts of the story inspire us. The bad parts warn us of what we have to do to make things better. Even though many Western films have only a slight connection to the true history of the West, I believe exposure to these motion pictures can stimulate kids to learn more about what their forefathers endured to make the United States one nation, from sea to shining sea.

I wish the kids of today knew more about the early pioneers and what they went through: rugged trails, starvation, traveling in terrible conditions of weather and in constant danger. I wish kids knew how the forests were conquered and the mountains were crossed, how families had to live for months in covered wagons, enduring great hardships, even death.

Western films and television programs can help to introduce this rich, colorful history, and I am heartened every time I see that a new Western has been made.

(From *I Was That Masked Man*, by Moore and Thompson)

a nation dedicated not to power but to ideals. In that sense, the U.S. needs heroes more than ever. (*TIME*, June 24, 1966).

To the extent this observation is true, we need heroes today who are heroes because of the ideas they champion. The next question is what – or whose – ideas? As we have seen, the early TV western heroes offered a set of ideas to be championed.

In the 1950s, and on into the 1960s, the television western program was considered by many critics as essentially a morality play in American culture. Referring to the then-popular television western shows, a psychologist compared them to the morality plays developed in many cultures and noted that both in the western and "in the morality play, pure virtue is extolled and some of this virtue rubs off on an audience waiting to be reminded that these are the only worthwhile and eternal moral values." (*Broadcasting-Telecasting*, September 2, 1957). So if a western is a morality play, extolling certain virtues or values, of particular concern should be who or what is the source of those values? On whose authority are virtues declared as such?

Cowboy Codes and the Ten Commandments

Throughout history, some inner sense of right and wrong has inspired people to be accountable to a higher moral standard or authority. In ancient history, some leaders and teachers known for having codified principles of conscience and ethics included iconic names like Moses, Confucius, Lao Tsu, Hammurabi, and others. The need for a standard originating from a higher level of authority has seemingly been recognized from the beginning. An atheist may prefer to deny the existence of any divine power, while insisting man is free – collectively and individually – to make and live by one's personally-derived set of morals. However, if they are honest, they must acknowledge such an approach does not work in a practical application at the societal level in real life.

The rules in life that carry the most authority are those derived from a divine source to whom all are accountable. At a personal level, one cannot validate or establish their authority or ideas by appealing only to their self as that would be more or less circular reasoning – sort of like the parental statement all children dread, "because I said so!" The validation of one's authority must derive from an even more-validated source. As we have seen, the cowboy codes and creeds contained strong moral values that inherently – and explicitly – acknowledged a higher authority to which all are accountable. Their codes had significance because they applied to everyone – not just cowboys.

It is no mere coincidence that the cowboy codes and creeds usually each consisted of ten articles. In 1949, still at the beginning of the television age, more than half of the American population (53%) claimed to belong to a religious group, with 99% of them identifying as Protestant, Catholic, or Jewish. Church attendance was strong as Americans were open to religious guidance to cope with the issues of the day. *Quick* magazine, in their New Year's Day 1951 issue, reported: "The mid-century religious revival in America is spreading rapidly, . . . Fearing an atomic war and losing faith in substitutes for religion (statism, science), Americans are boosting church attendances to record highs (81 million). Other signs: popularity of religious books; more college courses in religion; growing popularity of Bible meetings." (*Quick*, January 1, 1951). Thus, given the degree of familiarity in the culture with Biblical teachings, most viewers would readily make the connection between the Ten Commandments and a cowboy's ten-point code.

The cowboy codes, like the Ten Commandments, were made up of articles that instruct us on how to best govern our relationships with each other (and to God). New Testament passages such as found in Romans 13:9-10 indicate that the Old Testament Law – of which the Ten Commandments were a part – was given to help man know how to show love toward both God and each other. Here is a listing of the Old Testament's Ten Commandments, in abbreviated form.

1. You shall have no other gods before Me.
2. You shall not make idols.
3. You shall not take the name of the LORD your God in vain.
4. Remember the Sabbath day, to keep it holy.
5. Honor your father and your mother.
6. You shall not murder.
7. You shall not commit adultery.
8. You shall not steal.
9. You shall not bear false witness against your neighbor.
10. You shall not covet.

(See Exodus 20:1-17 and Deuteronomy 5:6-21).

These Ten Commandments have served as a basis for our standard of morality and our collective sense of right and wrong for centuries. They were also the basis of English common law, which was the basis on which American law was developed.

> "Stand by the roads, and look, and ask for the ancient paths, where the good way is; and walk in it, and find rest for your souls."
>
> *(Jeremiah 6:16, ESV)*

Common Ground of Major Religions

The recognition of a higher authority is inherent in the B Western cowboy codes and creeds. This appeal to a higher power and universal truths is what actually gives them any validity at all. With or without access to and knowledge of the Bible, people who lived in ancient times seem to have intuitively felt the need to be subject to authority for the benefit of all. There was a willingness to embrace a common moral standard for the purpose of making decisions.

Others have previously observed that there exists a common core of values found within the teachings and commands of the world's major religions. This commonality is also found in the cowboy codes we have reviewed, and can be summarized by two essential statements: 1) Do all you have agreed you will do; and, 2) Do no harm to another's person or their property. The reader can see that these two statements represent a restatement of the Golden Rule. That these principles are common throughout all the major religions should be no surprise to us today. In the Bible, specifically found in the book of Romans, for example, we are told that even for those without the Law of Moses, God's Laws are written on the hearts of men.

A hallmark of the B western heroes was their decisiveness and certainty in determining a course of action. For example, when confronted with a challenge, the Lone Ranger typically was ready to act immediately and rallied those around him with the words, "now, here's my plan..." These cowboys seemed to always know the right thing to do, and felt compelled to act accordingly. Unlike the early television B westerns, the later "adult" western programs would specialize in dramas portraying characters who were struggling with their moral choices – even, at times, the "good guys." Today, while we still tend to easily decide between obvious good and evil, our modern society struggles with the difficulty in discerning the best choice when its options are between multiple "good" options.

Without a moral compass based on a faith in a higher authority, the desire for such clarity in decision-making will often elude even our best efforts. In a 1999 article in *American Cowboy* magazine, the writer concluded that the cowboy codes were not really about "cowboying," they were about something deeper – in particular, the nature and role of authority in a civilized society:

> That's what authority is, or what it does for us. It recognizes everything has its place, its natural order. It has faith that life has answers, not just potentialities or decisions. There's more to authority than just God over family and country. There's the authority of elder over younger, learned over unlearned, provider over provided for, defender over defended, the many over the individual, the accumulate wisdom of the centuries over the notions of one generation. (*American Cowboy*, September/October, 1999).

Learning the Rules and the Influence of Television Heroes

With each new innovation in the electronic age, the appetite of children for entertainment has proven to be quite insatiable. Modern readers are familiar with the now-common sight of youngsters moving about with their attention focused on their handheld electronic devices. The addiction to non-stop stimuli via the ability to access one's favorite music, video, and social media-of-the-day internet apps seems to be a reality to which the youth are perfectly adapted. This is not really a phenomenon unique to today's world, however. Beginning in the 1920s, kids could go to the nearest movie theater and watch exciting action on a big screen. Then radio came along and, within the comfort of their own homes, children could tune in to nerve-rattling, action-packed programs on a daily basis. Then, in the late-1940s, television finally arrived and children were suddenly found to be spending several additional hours per week squinting in spell-bound manner at a relatively small television screen and a flickering image received via often-weak, easily-distorted, broadcast signals.

Even for adults who grew up with television, it is easy now to forget how limited their television viewing options were in the 1950s. Most TV markets across the country had only two or three network-affiliated stations, with perhaps an additional signal from a local independent station.

Programming was correspondingly limited, and therefore, somewhat uniform across the country. This allowed television to quickly assume the role of a sort of cultural institution, acquiring the ability to powerfully communicate values and ideas to the vast numbers of young viewers tuning in.

The B western cowboys took advantage of the opportunity afforded by television to share their values with the juvenile audience. As children tuned in faithfully to follow the adventures of their favorite cowboy hero, they were learning – perhaps subconsciously most of the time – the importance of obeying the law, and standing up for the rights of one's fellow citizens, and all the other values embraced by Roy, Gene, Hoppy, the Lone Ranger, and all the other cowboy heroes.

Following All The Rules Is Difficult

As the young viewers of early TV westerns matured, so did their viewing tastes with the arrival of the immensely popular "adult" westerns on television. In the mid-to-late 1950s, shows like *Cheyenne*, *Gunsmoke*, *Maverick*, *Have Gun – Will Travel*, *The Rifleman*, and *Wagon Train* began to appear on the screen, and the popularity of the new westerns, as determined by the Nielsen ratings, soared to the point that adult western programming dominated the TV landscape. In March, 1959, *TIME* magazine reported:

> Last week eight of the top ten shows on TV were horse operas. The networks have saddled up no fewer than 35 of the bangtail brigade, and 30 of them are riding the dollar-green range of prime night time (from 7:30 to 10 p.m.). Independent stations too have taken to the field with every wring-tailed old oat snorter they could rustle out of Hollywood's back pasture. This season, while other shows, from quizzes to comedies, were dropping right and left like well-rehearsed Indians, not a single western left the air. Indeed, 14 new ones were launched, and the networks are planning more for next year. (*TIME*, March 30, 1959).

The article also reported that tie-in sales of toys suggested by TV westerns were expected to reach the $125 million level for the year.

The "adult" westerns represented a departure from the idealistic nature of the B westerns. As we all know, life is complicated, and the "adult" westerns attempted to depict this in their stories. We know there are rules in life, but living by those rules can be a difficult thing. The "adult" westerns thus featured stories that attempted to counter-balance the action-driven format of the B western heroes with more emphasis on realism, characterization, and in some cases, historical trappings. *Gunsmoke* was the leader in the "adult" western genre, and the show's producer, Norman Macdonnell, explained the show's differentiation from the B western format: "We never do action for action's sake. For instance, we've never had a chase on *Gunsmoke*. ... And cowboy speech isn't full of things like 'shucks' and 'side-winding varmint.'" (*TIME*, March 4, 1957).

The hero in the "adult" western – or some of them at least – was a character that more closely resembled the historical westerner, possessing fewer of the all-around heroic abilities of the B western heroes. For example, given the nature of the pistols most cowboys actually used in the late-1800s, only a few exceptional gunmen were actually masters of the quick-draw that so many western shows liked to portray. The typical westerner could not fire a pistol accurately beyond a range of 20 feet – a fact more accurately represented in the "adult" westerns than in the B westerns.

The heroes in these westerns also made mistakes sometimes, and they were not always pure in behavior or motive. With the "adult" western, the hero began to be seen routinely confronted with the difficulty in the struggles between good and evil, and the need to make a moral choice. The hero's judgment was not always perfect, and personal weaknesses were often visible. In some ways, "adult" westerns provided heroes who were more like us – flawed characters. It is interesting at this point to note that the heroes in the Bible were always presented as real-life people – including their flaws. The Biblical accounts of iconic figures like Abraham and Moses include their mistakes as well as their great deeds.

Handling decision-making in "gray" areas is not easy for any of us, but heroes have done so whenever they have been guided by fundamentally-sound moral values. A hero can be imperfect and yet make good decisions. This is a trait legendary filmmaker Steven Spielberg prefers in his film heroes – a person who acts with moral clarity. The maker of movies based in American history, like *Saving Private Ryan*, *Amistad*, and *Schindler's List*, Spielberg was quoted in a 2015 *TIME* magazine article about the heroes featured in his films: "I love characters who stand on their principles. I have to go into almost ancient history. It just feels to me like those times were simpler and there was no media clutter to put too many areas of gray into a righteous decision." (*TIME*, October 19, 2015).

Fortunately, heroes do not have to be perfect to serve effectively as role models. Biblical heroes like Noah, Abraham, Jacob, Joseph, Moses, Samson, David, and many more, were all imperfect men who managed to do the right thing more often than not, guided by a strong sense of moral values. The youngsters of today can still do well to follow the examples of these – and other historical – heroes because of what they stood for as much or more than their deeds. In the New Testament, we see an example of pointing others to a contemporary person as a role model when John singled out Demetrius as a man who was living an honorable life and as a good example for others to emulate. (See 3 John 1:11-12).

The Motive Behind a Hero's Actions

Anyone can be a "hero" in real life to some one or more of the people in their life. Doing so, however, requires having the moral values needed to properly guide one's decision-making and behavior. The early 1950s B western television heroes knew the importance of their actions being seen as motivated by virtue, and thus made available to their fans the codes and creeds we have examined. Yet, even in these early westerns – aimed primarily at a juvenile audience – innocent people were hurt or killed, normal people gave in to temptations that lead to criminal behavior, and hard-working families still faced financial problems. In each episode of these shows, the hero made the point that even in bad circumstances one must persevere by doing what is right.

During the 1950s and 1960s, there were programs such as *Fury*, *Lassie*, *National Velvet*, *Flipper*, *Gentle Ben*, and *Rin Tin Tin*, also aimed at the juvenile audience, that were similar in nature to the early B westerns and that reflected the same values. In these shows, through the combination of adult authority figures and heroic animals, the youthful central characters would be seen experiencing adventures from which they learned important lessons about life. Typical "lessons" involved plots centered around learning to be a responsible citizen, helping others, overcoming challenges in relationships with one's family members and friends, respect for parents, respect for nature, caring for animals, conserving natural resources, and that even a young person can make a difference by doing the right thing.

However, knowing one's moral code and then "doing what is right" is easy to acknowledge as one's goal, but often proves challenging to actually do. So what makes us want to even try to adhere to any particular creed or code? Perhaps the real basis for a hero's actions is something that is even more fundamental to their character. Claiming a code of conduct is great as far as it goes, but what is the real motivation for actually doing the right thing?

For the answer to that question, we can turn to the words of Jesus in Matthew 7:12 (NLT), where we read that the essence of all the commandments is to "do to others whatever you would like them to do to you." The writer in Galatians 5:14 (ESV) summarized it this way: "For the whole law is fulfilled in one word: 'You shall love your neighbor as yourself.'"

So it would appear that love is an important motivating force at work in properly living out the virtues and values propagated in all the codes and creeds. The apostle Paul made the connection between love and the commandments quite clear in Romans 13, in which he stated that any commandment derives its value from a basis of love:

> Owe no man any thing, but to love one another: for he that loveth another hath fulfilled the law. For this, Thou shalt not commit adultery, Thou shalt not kill, Thou shalt not steal, Thou shalt not bear false witness, Thou shalt not covet; and if there be any other commandment, it is briefly comprehended in this saying, namely, Thou shalt love thy neighbour as thyself. Love worketh no ill to his neighbour: therefore love is the fulfilling of the law. (Romans 13:8-10, KJV).

By a similar reasoning, and based on teachings originating from a higher authority, love is the fulfilling of the cowboy codes, creeds, and commandments examined in this book. Dale Evans included these same themes in a song she penned for an episode of *The Roy Rogers Show*: "Have faith, hope, and charity / that's the way to live successfully / how do I know, the Bible tells me so." Why else would Roy, Gene, Hoppy, the Lone Ranger, or any other hero, work so hard to do the right thing?

EPILOGUE

In reflecting upon the actions of the heroes of the early TV B westerns, we can see how they behaved in a manner consistent with the Golden Rule. Furthermore, we have seen that within their codes and creeds is an acknowledgement – both implicit and explicit – that such values are derived from a source they knew to be greater than themselves. They were heroes, but not super-heroes. They were heroes because they were human beings coming to the aid of their fellow man.

The cowboy heroes of early 1950s television attracted large numbers of fans because they provided fun action-based entertainment and because they represented likeable individuals who consistently chose to stand for truth and fairness. The B westerns of television provided a perfect platform to showcase this kind of hero. When speaking of the cowboy hero of the American West, Armie Hammer, the actor who portrayed the Lone Ranger in the 2013 Disney movie, observed:

> Everything is 100 percent on you. You are free in a way that people in other places, in other countries, don't understand. You have the freedom to be the good guy or bad guy if you choose, and because you have that, you choose to do the responsible thing, and sometimes you're tested. It's the true American West we all love. (*American Cowboy*, retrieved 1/12/2015 from *American Cowboy* website at http://www.americancowboy.com/article/lone-ranger-rides-again).

The youngsters in the viewing audience knew they too could make the individual choice to do the right thing – just like their favorite on-screen cowboy or cowgirl. The vast amount of merchandise they purchased gave them a chance to role-play exactly those things in their own back yards.

As noted at the beginning of this book, the cowboy codes, creeds, commandments, and rules to live by, were meant to apply to all of us. They express values and virtues that are universal, and are as valid today as when they were first published. As a closing to our review of these codes and creeds, consider these remarks about the legacy left by Roy Rogers:

> In his films and in the messages he's given us, though they may seem innocent and simplistic to modern audiences, he left behind a legacy. The code of conduct he prescribed for boys and girls was just one example. Good advice for little cowboys and cowgirls. Or big ones. Or the whole human race, for that matter. (*American Cowboy*, September/October 1998).

APPENDIX

While the individual B-western heroes' creeds and codes considered in this book varied in detail, they actually highlighted several common themes – as summarized in the chart below.

Theme	Roy Rogers Riders Club Rules and Creed	Gene Autry's Cowboy Code of Honor	Hopalong Cassidy's Creed for American Boys and Girls	The Lone Ranger Creed	The Wild Bill Hickok Deputy Marshal's Code of Conduct	The Texas Rangers "Deputy Ranger" Oath	Bobby Benson Rider's Pledge	The Straight Shooters' Pledge	Buck Jones Cowboy Creed
Exhibit clean/healthy behavior in body, thought, word, and actions.	✓	✓	✓		✓	✓	✓	✓	✓
Be a good worker/student, who is diligent in work/study.	✓	✓	✓	✓	✓			✓	✓
With the proper attitude, be ready and willing to help the weak and those in need/trouble.	✓	✓	✓	✓	✓	✓	✓		✓
Trust/believe in God, and regularly attend church/place of worship.	✓			✓	✓	✓	✓		
Obey one's parents.	✓	✓	✓		✓	✓		✓	✓
Be patriotic. Obey our nation's laws.	✓	✓	✓	✓	✓	✓	✓		
Respectful care/treatment of animals.	✓	✓	✓		✓				
Be respectful/act with integrity toward others, regardless of race, ethnicity, age, religion.	✓	✓	✓	✓	✓	✓		✓	✓
Be wise in the handling of one's money, time, resources	✓		✓	✓					

RESOURCES CONSULTED

Books and Articles

"A Day at Disneyland (Spring Byington and Bobby Diamond on a wonderland visit)." *Radio TV Mirror*, April, 1956.

"A Dog's Life (Lassie)." *Radio TV Mirror*, September, 1957.

"Advertest Survey Measures Popularity of Westerns on TV." *Sponsor*, May 21, 1951.

Advertisement. *Radio and Television Mirror*, October, 1948.

Advertisement. *Radio and Television Mirror*, February, 1950.

Advertisement. *Radio TV Mirror*, February, 1955.

Advertisement. *TV Guide*, October 8, 1955.

Advertisement. *TV Guide*, October 13, 1956.

Advertisement: "Ride to adventure with "The Cisco Kid" at 7 p.m." *TV Guide*, July 8, 1967.

Advertisement: "Western Roundup." *Sponsor*, October 8, 1951.

"Agency Ad Libs." *Sponsor*, April 18, 1955.

Albert, Dora. "The World's My Family (Roy Rogers and Dale Evans)." *TV Radio Mirror*, February, 1957.

Alden, Ken. "Facing the Music." *Radio Mirror*, June, 1943.

"Answer to Prayer (Roy Rogers." *TV Radio Mirror*, May, 1955.

Autry, Gene. "Gene Autry Prize Round-Up." *Radio Television Mirror*, July, 1951.

------------. "Outlaw Boy." *Radio Mirror*, October, 1946.

------------. "Rhythm of the Hoofbeats: Words and music of twin song hits by a popular singing cowboy." *Radio and Television Mirror*, February, 1941.

Banks, Dale. "What's New from Coast to Coast." *Radio Mirror*, November, 1943.

-----------. "What's New from Coast to Coast." *Radio Mirror*, January, 1947.

-----------. "What's New from Coast to Coast." *Radio and Television Mirror*, May, 1948.

-----------. "What's New from Coast to Coast." *Radio and Television Mirror*, August, 1948.

-----------. "What's New from Coast to Coast." *Radio and Television Mirror*, October, 1948.

-----------. "What's New from Coast to Coast." *Radio and Television Mirror*, March, 1949.

Bets, Mary. "For Love of Melinda (Groucho Marx)." *Radio-TV Mirror*, May, 1953.

Blair, Dorothy. "Come and Visit Roy Rogers." *Radio and Television Mirror*, August, 1949.

"Bobby Benson Arrives for Lewiston Roundup." *Spokane Daily Chronicle*, September 10, 1954.

Bolstad, Helen. "New Hot Singers of 1957." *TV Radio Mirror*, August, 1957.

Borie, Marcia. "The Magic Steed (Lori Martin)." *Radio TV Mirror*, October, 1960.

*Broadcasting*Telecasting*, February 27, 1956.

Broadcasting, February 20, 1950.

Broadcasting, June 7, 1954.

Broadcasting, March 3, 1952.

Broadcasting, March 8, 1954.

Broadcasting, May 17, 1948.

Broadcasting, May 18, 1953.

Broadcasting, September 25, 1950.

Bronski, Peter. "The Lone Ranger Rides Again." *American Cowboy*, retrieved 1/12/2015 from American Cowboy.com.

Budge, Gordon. "Keeping Up With The Joneses." *Radio TV Mirror*, September, 1957.

------------. "Almost Like Angels (Bill Williams and Barbara Hale)." *Radio TV Mirror*, August, 1957.

"Buffalo Bill, Jr." *TV Guide*, July 2, 1955.

"Business & Finance: Moppets' Stampede." *Time*, Aug 29, 1949.

"Business." *Quick*, April 10, 1950.

"Business: Wanna' Buy a Radio Show?" *Quick*, April 9, 1951.

Butler, Helen. "Meet the MacMullans." *Radio Television Mirror*, June, 1951.

"Coast to Coast in Television." *Radio and Television Mirror*, March, 1949.

"Coast to Coast." *Radio Television Mirror*, March, 1951.

"Come and Visit Perry Como." *Radio Mirror*, July, 1947.

"Come and Visit Andy." *Radio and Television Mirror*, March, 1949.

"Costs Fly Thataway (Up) for TV Westerns." *Broadcasting*, August 27, 1956.

Cron, John B. "Film Notes and Trends." *Sponsor*, April 5, 1954.

D'Addario, Daniel. "For Two Legends, History Is Personal." *TIME*, October 19, 2015.

Denenberg, Dennis and Lorraine Roscoe. *50 American Heroes Every Kid Should Meet*. Minneapolis: Millbrook Press, 2005.

Dichter, Ph. D., Ernest. "Why They Keep on Going Thataway: Psychologist defends westerns as native art form of real permanence." *Broadcasting*Telecasting*, September 2, 1957.

Dunning, John. *On the Air – The Encyclopedia of Old-Time Radio*. New York, NY: Oxford University Press, Inc., 1998.

"Editor's Note." *Radio and Television Mirror*, March, 1949.

Edwards, Ralph. "What Makes a Person Interesting?" *TV Radio Mirror*, March, 1956.

"Education: The Violent & the Bland." *Time*, August 6, 1956.

"Entertainers: Him Mingo." *TIME*, September 29, 1967.

"Entertainment: Television in the News." *Quick*, November 20, 1950.

Epstein, Marvin. "How TV Looks to the Third-Graders." *TV Guide*, September 25, 1953.

"Essay: ON THE DIFFICULTY OF BEING A CONTEMPORARY HERO." *TIME*, June 24, 1966.

Fannin, Cole. *Roy Rogers and Dale Evans in River of Peril*. Racine, WI: Whitman Publishing Company, 1957.

Ferguson, Ken and Sylvia, ed. *Western Stars of Television and Film*. 1967.

"Film Facts and Figures." *Sponsor*, January 23, 1956.

"Film notes and trends: Canada Dry builds free carton promotion around 'Annie Oakley'." *Sponsor*, May 3, 1954.

"Film report . . ." *Broadcasting*, September 10, 1951.

"Film-Scope." *Sponsor*, April 12, 1958.

"Film-Scope." *Sponsor*, March 28, 1959.

Fisher, George. "Hollywood Radio Whispers." *Radio and Television Mirror*, March, 1940.

------------. "Hollywood Radio Whispers." *Radio and Television Mirror*, June, 1940.

------------. "Hollywood Radio Whispers." *Radio and Television Mirror*, August, 1940.

"Four of a Kind." *Sponsor*, May 2, 1955.

Francis, Alice. "You Showed Me the Way (Gene Autry)." *Radio-TV Mirror*, April, 1954.

"Frontiers: For God, Family, and Country – Revisited - Why cowboy codes are not about cowboying." *American Cowboy*, September/October, 1999.

"Gene Autry: Richest Cowboy." *Quick*, December 5, 1949.

Glickman, Dave. "Hollywood Talent." *Broadcasting*Telecasting*, August 13, 1951.

Goode, Bud. "Golden Girl (Annie Oakley)." *Radio TV Mirror*, January, 1957.

----------. "What's New on the West Coast." *Radio TV Mirror*, September, 1957.

Grams, Jr., Martin and Terry Salomonson. *The Green Hornet: A History of Radio, Motion Pictures, Comics, and Television*. Churchville, MD: OTR Publishing, L.L.C, 2010.

Hanauer, Joan. "Disney Productions Revives the Western." *Chicago Tribune*, March 17, 1985.

"He Just Keeps Ridin' Along on TV: Syndicated Roy Rogers' re-runs bring big results for Nestle." *Broadcasting*, July 18, 1960.

"He's Not Just Acting! (Roy Rogers)." *Radio-TV Mirror*, May, 1954.

Henty, G.A. *Redskin and Cow-Boy, A Tale of the Western Plains*. New York: Charles Scribner's Sons, 1896.

Hollis, Tim. *Hi There, Boys and Girls!: America's Local Children's TV Programs*. Jackson: University Press of Mississippi, 2001.

"Home In The Hills." *Radio and Television Mirror*, October, 1950.

"Hooray for Gene Autry!" *TV Radio Mirror*, May, 1956.

"Hopalong Cassidy: Cowboy in the Parlor." *Quick*, May 1, 1950.

"How They Make Superman Fly." *TV Guide*, September 25, 1953.

"How TV took a candy out of the doldrums." *Sponsor*, June 16, 1952.

"In Review – Wild Bill Hickok." *Broadcasting*, June 13, 1955.

"Information Booth." *Radio-TV Mirror*, February, 1952.

"Information Booth." *TV Radio Mirror*, August, 1954.

"Information Booth." *TV Radio Mirror*, December, 1954.

"Information Booth." *Radio TV Mirror*, June, 1955.

"Information Booth." *Radio TV Mirror*, April, 1956.

"Information Booth." *Radio TV Mirror*, March, 1956.

"Information Booth." *Radio TV Mirror*, February, 1956.

"Information Booth." *Radio TV Mirror*, June, 1959.

Jenkins, Dan. "Why Roy Rogers Is Cowboy King." *TV Guide*, July 17, 1954.

Jenkins, Dan. "TV Teletype." *TV Guide*, July 2, 1955.

Jensen, Oliver. "Hopalong Hits the Jackpot." *LIFE*, June 12, 1950.

"Junior Mirror." *Radio-TV Mirror*, October, 1951.

"Junior Mirror." *Radio-TV Mirror*, September, 1951.

"Kellogg Revises Lineup For 'Hickok' and 'Superman'." *Broadcasting*Telecasting*, July 12, 1954.

"King of the Cowboys." *Quick*, February 20, 1950.

Lansing, Joan. "Have You Heard?" *Radio and Television Mirror*, August, 1950.

-------------. "Have You Seen?" *Radio and Television Mirror*, December, 1950.

-------------. "Have You Heard?" *Radio and Television Mirror*, January, 1951.

"'Lone Ranger' Sets Record." *Broadcasting*, August 1, 1949.

"MANNERS & MORALS: Kiddies in the Old Corral." *Time*, Nov. 27, 1950.

Marsano, William. "Where Are They Now? The Cisco Kid and the Continental – 15 years later." *TV Guide*, November 21, 1970.

Maybury, Richard J. *Whatever Happened to Justice?* Placerville, CA: Bluestocking Press, 2004.

Miller, Llewellyn. "Radio's Own Life Story." *Radio and Television Mirror*, July, 1950.

Mills, Betty. "Romance Is Forever (Gene Autry)." *Radio-TV Mirror*, December, 1952.

------------. "*Kit Carson* Finds His Mate (Bill Williams)." *Radio TV Mirror*, January, 1955.

Molina, Elsa. "Alias Zorro (Guy Williams)." *TV Radio Mirror*, January, 1958.

Moore, Clayton and Frank Thompson. *I Was That Masked Man*. New York: Taylor Trade Publishing, 1998.

Moore, Viola. "Hopalong Cassidy Hangs His Hat." *Radio-TV Mirror*, April, 1952.

Mullins, Jesse. "He'll Always Be King of the Cowboys." *American Cowboy*, September/October 1998.

Nelson, Harriet Hilliard. "Bringing Up the Boys," *Radio and Television Mirror*, January, 1949.

"Never say a bad word about an Indian." *Broadcasting*, October 17, 1960.

"New Developments on SPONSOR Stories." *Sponsor*, July 17, 1950.
"New Developments on Sponsor Stories." *Sponsor*, May 7, 1951.
"No Wonder the Younger Set Loves TV." *TV Guide*, October 8, 1955.
"Not Sponsored – But Big Business (How Mutual's Bobby Benson sells 40 products in carload lots with benefit of advertiser)." *Sponsor*, May 22, 1950.
O'Neal, Bill. "King of the Cowboys Roy Rogers once ruled television, movies, and the airwaves with charisma and a clear, melodic voice." *American Cowboy*, retrieved 1/12/2015 from American Cowboy.com.
"Opinion from Columnists." *Quick*, December 5, 1949.
Oppenheimer, Peer J. "Winsome *Annie Oakley* (Gail Davis)." *Radio TV Mirror*, September, 1955.
"Outdoor Man (Roy Rogers)." *TV Radio Mirror*, May, 1957.
Parker, William. "Television for Children." *Radio Television Mirror*, July, 1951.
Parks, Annette. "Bert's a Perfect Father." *Radio-TV Mirror*, January, 1952.
Pinkerton, Jane. *Broadcasting Magazine*, March 23, 1953.
"Program Highlights in Television Viewing." *Radio Television Mirror*, May, 1951.
"Program Highlights in Television Viewing." *Radio Television Mirror*, June, 1951.
"Program Highlights in Television Viewing." *Radio Television Mirror*, July, 1951.
"Program Highlights in Television Viewing." *Radio Television Mirror*, August, 1951.
"Program Highlights in Television Viewing." *Radio Television Mirror*, September, 1951.
"Program Highlights in Television Viewing." *Radio Television Mirror*, October, 1951.
"Program Highlights in Television Viewing." *Radio Television Mirror*, November, 1951.
"Program Highlights in Television Viewing." *Radio Television Mirror*, December, 1951.
"Program Highlights in Television Viewing." *Radio-TV Mirror*, January, 1952.
R.S. "Annie Oakley." *TV Guide*, May 7, 1954.
Radio and Television Mirror, January, 1950.
Radio and Television Mirror, July, 1941.
"Radio: Audience Reaction." *Time*, February 9, 1953.
"Radio: Old Plot, New Angle." *Time*, July 31, 1950.
"Radio: The Week in Review." *Time*, Oct 18, 1954.
"Radio: The Masked Rider." *Time*, January 14, 1952.
"Radio: The Week in Review." *TIME*, December 12, 1955.
"Random Shots." *Broadcasting*, July 6, 1953.
"Religion Stirs U.S." *Quick*, January 1, 1951.
"Religion: Americans Are Churchgoers." *Quick*, Sept. 5, 1949.
"Religion: Sunday Double-Feature." *Quick*, April 2, 1951.
Rettig, Mrs. Rosemary. "He Loves a *Lassie* (Tommy Rettig)." *Radio TV Mirror*, October, 1955.
"Reviews: Brave Eagle." *TV Guide*, January 14-20, 1956.
Rinker, Harry L. *Hopalong Cassidy – King of the Cowboy Merchandisers*. Atglen, PA: Schiffer Publishing, Ltd., 1995.
---------------. "RINKER ON COLLECTIBLES." *The Morning Call*, August 09, 1998.
Rogers, Roy, Dale Evans, Jane Stern, and Michael Stern . *Happy Trails: Our Life Story*. New York: Simon and Schuster Inc., 1994.
Rothel, David. *The Gene Autry Book*. Madison, NC: Empire Publishing Company, Inc., 1988.
-------------. *The Roy Rogers Book*. Madison, NC: Empire Publishing, Inc., 1988.
Roy Rogers Enterprises. "Riders Club Rules and Creed." *Official Roy Rogers Riders Club Comics*, 1952.
"Roy Rogers Shoots for Santa." *LIFE*, November 16, 1953.
"Roy Rogers Dreams of Santa." *LIFE*, November 15, 1954.
"Roy Rogers to Headline 1952 World Championship Rodeo." *TV Life*, July 12-18, 1952.
Royal, John F. "What About Television?" *Radio Mirror*, 1946.

Santo, Avi. *Selling the Silver Bullet: The Lone Ranger and Transmedia Brand Licensing*. Austin, TX: University of Texas Press, 2015.

"Sensational but Scarce." *Sponsor*, June 5, 1950.

Senseney, Dan. "What's New From Coast to Coast." *Radio and Television Mirror*, August, 1940.

------------. "What's New from Coast to Coast." *Radio Mirror*, December, 1938.

"Show Business: The Busy Air." *TIME*, November 24, 1958.

Silver, Alexandra. "Fess Parker." *TIME*, April 5, 2010.

Sponsor, July 30, 1951.

Stahl, Bob. "TV Teletype." *TV Guide*, September 25, 1953.

"Steve Allen's Turntable." *TV Radio Mirror*, January, 1956.

Sullivan, Ed. "Radio Television Mirror Awards Winners for 1950." *Radio Television Mirror*, May, 1951.

------------. "Radio Television Mirror Awards Winners for 1950." *Radio Television Mirror*, May, 1951.

"'Superman' Deal: Flamingo Gets Rights." *Broadcasting*Telecasting*, May 14, 1951.

Swanson, Pauline. "If You Were Mrs. Gene Autry: A glimpse into the home of radio's singing cowboy." *Radio and Television Mirror*, May, 1941.

Television Age, August 1953.

"Television Highlights." *Radio and Television Mirror*, July, 1950.

Television Magazine, April 1953.

Television Magazine, July 1953.

Television Magazine, July 1954.

Television Magazine, May 1956.

Television Magazine, Sept 1956.

Television Magazine, Nov 1957.

"Television." *Radio Mirror*, January, 1948.

"Television: High in the Saddle." *TIME*, March 4, 1957.

"TELEVISION: O Sage Can You See." *TIME*, November 3, 1958.

"Television: Up." *Quick*, March 27, 1950.

Temple, Mary. "They Count Their Blessings (Roy Rogers and Dale Evans)." *TV Radio Mirror*, January, 1956.

Terrace, Vincent. *Television Introductions: Narrated TV Program Openings since 1949*. Lanham, MD: Scarecrow Press, Inc., 2014.

"Thanks, Pardner! (Gene Autry)." *Radio-TV Mirror*, May, 1955.

"The Children's Hour." *Sponsor*, November, 1947.

"The Cisco's Kids." *TV Guide*, August 13, 1955.

"The Cowboy and His Lady (Gene Autry)." *Radio-TV Mirror*, May, 1954.

"The Lone Ranger." *Radio Mirror*, May, 1943.

"The Lone Ranger." *Radio-TV Mirror*, February, 1952.

"The Lone Ranger Rides Again…this time for the U.S. Treasury." *TV Guide*, October 18-24, 1958.

"The Mystery of the Lone Ranger." *Radio Mirror*, September, 1938.

"The new NBC-TV weekly series." *Broadcasting*, September 28, 1959.

"These Animals Aren't So Dumb!" *TV Guide*, July 2, 1955.

"TV Captures the Kids." *Sponsor*, September 26, 1949.

"TV FILM GETS HOLLYWOOD EXPLOITATION TREATMENT." *Television Magazine*, July 1952.

"TV films – Picture organizations learning art of producing air film for sponsors." *Sponsor*, July 18, 1949.

"TV HOMES HIT 19.5 MILLION IN 1952." *Broadcasting*, April 13, 1953.

TV Life, April 26-May 2, 1952.

"TV Production." *Sponsor*, March 10, 1952.

"TV Program Listings", *Radio Television Mirror*, April, 1951.

"TV Program Highlights." *Radio-TV Mirror*, February, 1952.

"TV Program Listings." *Radio-TV Mirror*, March, 1952.

"TV Program Listings." *Radio-TV Mirror*, April, 1952.
"TV Program Listings." *Radio-TV Mirror*, November, 1952.
"TV Radio Mirror Award Winners, 1956-57." *TV Radio Mirror*, May, 1957.
"TV Radio Mirror Award Winners, 1954-55." *TV Radio Mirror*, May, 1955.
"TV Results: Hopalong Novelties." *Sponsor*, November 5, 1951.
"TV Teletype." *TV Guide*, May 7, 1954.
"Two for All (Roy Rogers and Dale Evans)." *TV Radio Mirror*, May, 1956.
"Unrest in the Air." *Radio and Television Mirror*, March, 1949.
Valentry, Duane. "That Old Family Feeling (Roy Rogers and Dale Evans)." *Radio-TV Mirror*, June, 1952.
Verral, Charles Spain. *The Lone Ranger and Tonto*. New York: Simon and Schuster, 1957.
Warren, Jill. "What's New from Coast to Coast." *Radio-TV Mirror*, December, 1953.
------------. "What's New from Coast to Coast." *Radio-TV Mirror*, August, 1954.
------------. "What's New from Coast to Coast." *Radio-TV Mirror*, August, 1952.
------------. "What's New from Coast to Coast." *TV Radio Mirror*, August, 1954.
------------. "What's New from Coast to Coast." *Radio-TV Mirror*, July, 1954.
------------. "What's New from Coast to Coast." *TV Radio Mirror*, December, 1954.
------------. "What's New from Coast to Coast." *Radio RV Mirror*, December, 1955.
------------. "What's New from Coast to Coast." *Radio TV Mirror*, August, 1956.
Waterbury, Ruth. "He Believes in Kids." *Radio and Television Mirror*, February, 1950.
"Westerns: The Six-Gun Galahad." *Time*, March 30, 1959.
"What Do You Want to Know?" *Radio and Television Mirror*, October, 1940.
White, Raymond E. *King of the Cowboys Queen of the West*. Madison, WI: Popular Press, 2005.
Whiteman, Paul. "TV-and Your Children." *Radio and Television Mirror*, September, 1950.
Whitney, Dwight. "The Inside Story of Hopalong Cassidy." *Coronet!*, December, 1950.
"Who's who in Radio-TV." *Radio-TV Mirror*, July, 1952.
"Wild-West Fever: Will It Sell for You?" *Sponsor*, September 11, 1950.
"Wild-West Fever: Will It Sell for You?, Part 2." *Sponsor*, September 25, 1950.
"World News." *Quick*, Nov. 5, 1951.
"Hi-Yo Silver!" *Movie-Radio Guide*, August, 1943.

Websites

biblehub.com
b-westerns.com
Carolynmappleton.wordpress.com
Chronicleoftheoldwest.com
Cowboyup.com
Dvdtalk.com
Elvaquero.com
Geneautry.com
Hopalong.com
kidshow.dcmemories.com
Legendsofamerica.com
martingrams.blogspot.com
Mtpioneer.com
old-time.com
otrarchive.blogspot.com
otrsite.com
Phantomranch.net
research.archives.gov

royrogersworld.com
sergeantpreston.com
Skyking.com
Tv-cowboys.com
tvobscurities.com
tvparty.com
Westernclippings.com
yesweekly.com

Video Recordings

All screenshots appearing in this book are taken from video recordings within the author's collection, including but not limited to:

"The Gene Autry Show: The Complete TV Series (Collector's Edition)," DVD, Shout!
    Factory / Timeless Media.
"Hopalong Cassidy: The Complete Television Series," DVD, Shout Factory.
"The Lone Ranger (Collector's Edition)," DVD, Classic Media.

Cover Images Credits

Front Cover Image: From an advertisement in a 1950s *Sponsor* magazine.
Back Cover Image: Screenshot from a promotional trailer for the Roy Rogers Riders Club.

Roy Rogers' prayer to be said at the beginning of each Riders Club meeting:

Lord, I reckon I'm not much just by myself,
I fail to do a lot of things I ought to do.
But Lord, when trails are steep and passes high,
Help me ride it straight the whole way through.
And when in the falling dusk I get that final call,
I do not care how many flowers they send,
Above all else, the happiest trail would be,
For You to say to me, "Let's ride, My Friend."
Amen.

(Retrieved 3/26/2015, from RoyRogersWorld.com, at url:
http://www.royrogersworld.com/TVShow.htm)

ABOUT THE AUTHOR

Matthew McKenzie has spent his professional career working as an analyst in the insurance industry. He currently resides with his family in the Winston-Salem area of North Carolina.

Creeds, Codes and Cowboy Commandments

www.ingramcontent.com/pod-product-compliance
Lightning Source LLC
LaVergne TN
LVHW011223080426
835509LV00005B/289